MW01591796

Keto Desserts
100+ Ketogenic Recipes to Help You Transition To a Ketogenic Diet

Richard Miller

Copyright © 2017 by Richard Miller

All rights reserved. This book or any portion thereof
may not be reproduced or used in any manner whatsoever
without the express written permission of the publisher
except for the use of brief quotations in a book review.

ISBN: 9781790282289
Imprint: Independently published

Table of Contents

Introduction

I am so excited that you have chosen to take a new path using the Ketogenic diet with the aid of the *Keto Desserts*. The following chapters will discuss how to follow the plan and the ways it will most benefit your health. If you take the approach of eating less without considering your diet, you could be losing essential minerals and vitamins you need daily. Unfortunately, this can result in muscle spasms, fatigue, mental fogginess, hunger, headaches, irritability, insomnia, and emotional depression. You can also lose valuable muscle mass—not just the pounds you intended to drop. The lifestyle change is worth the journey.

Stages of the Ketogenic Plan

This is an important step. You must decide how you want to proceed with your diet plan. It is always best to discuss this with your physician. These are the basics:

Method 1: Choose from the standard Ketogenic diet (SKD) which consists of high fat, moderate protein, and extremely low carbs.

Method 2: The cyclical Ketogenic diet (CKD) is created with 5 Keto days followed by 2 high-carbohydrate days.

Method 3: The high-protein Keto (HPK) diet is much like the SKD plan in all aspects, except that it has more protein.

Method 4: The targeted Keto diet (TKD) will provide you with a plan to add carbs to the diet during the times when you are working out.

If you are new to the Ketogenic way of eating, you will probably want to use the first method. You can range from 20 to 50 calories in one day. Hence, you may want to use your carbs wisely. Each of the recipes in this cookbook is calculated so that you will understand how much you can indulge with the delicious treats.

Before we get started, why not try a cup of Butter Coffee? Here is the Recipe:

Servings: 1
Macros: 0 g Net Carbs | 0 g Protein | 25 g Fat | 230 Cal.

Ingredients:

- Coffee – 2 tbsp.
- Water – 1 cup
- Grass-fed butter – 1 tbsp.
- Coconut oil – 1 tbsp.
- Useful: Turkish coffee pot or a regular pot

Preparation Method:

1. Prepare your coffee the way you like it. You can simmer ground coffee in water for five minutes and strain it into the cup.
2. Pour the coffee into a high-speed blender (for example – NutriBullet). Add the coconut, oil, and butter. Mix for about 10 seconds.
3. Pour it into a mug and relax. Add cinnamon or whipped cream (but count the carbs), and enjoy!

Now, that is just for starters. Just sit back and relax. If you are new to the diet plan, the first chapter will enlighten you for the basics. If you are a veteran, maybe there is something there for you as well.

Chapter 1: Essentials of the Ketogenic Diet

Just to get you on the right track for preparing your delicious desserts and special treats, this section will provide you a few essential guidelines.

The "Yes" Foods

To supplement your Ketogenic diet plan, refer to the following list. It will provide you with an abundance of "sweet" food choices included on the Keto diet. Experiment with your new recipes, and use this list as a guideline when you begin your dessert planning list:

Fats & Oils: Plan your fats from natural sources including nuts. It is best to supplement with saturated and monounsaturated fats—including butter, extra-virgin olive oil (EVOO), and similar items you will see throughout the diet plan cookbook.

Dairy Products: Choose dairy products that have been cultured and are Keto-friendly. Milk alone is high in carbs (lactose), unless its cultured and turned into the sour cream for example. You can also try dairy substitutes. The number one choice is unsweetened almond milk. You can also choose from hemp milk and flax milk.

Do you know the difference between butter and ghee? Butter consists of water, milk solids, and butterfat. On the other hand, ghee, an Indian staple, includes pure butterfat. Therefore, if you have lactose sensitivities, ghee is probably your best choice. The ghee also contains medium chain fatty acids, which assist your immune system and digestion.

Nuts & Seeds: Create some tasty meals (in moderation) when adding seeds and nuts to your Keto diet plan. Use fattier nuts including macadamias and almonds.

Lemon and Lime: Your blood sugar levels will naturally drop with these citric additions and signal a boost in your liver function. The choices are limitless and assist you with the following:

- Relieves respiratory infections
- Reduces toothache pain
- Boosts your immune system
- Balances pH
- Reduces fever
- Excellent for weight loss
- Blood purifier
- Decreases wrinkles and blemishes

Cinnamon: Use cinnamon as part of your daily plan to improve your insulin receptor activity. Just put one-half of a teaspoon of cinnamon into a shake or any type of Keto dessert. As you will see, many of the Keto recipes contain the ingredient.

A Note About Pumpkin: Include pumpkin in your 'must have' list even though it is considered a vegetable. It is full of essential minerals and vitamins including B1, B6, and PP. Carotenes are also in abundance with vitamin A. It has been noted that pumpkin is about 4.5 times higher in vitamin A than carrots. You will notice many of the dessert recipes will incorporate pumpkin into its list.

Low Carb Flours: As you begin your new and healthier lifestyle, you will discover many shortcuts or substitutes to help you stay on track. Some of these replacements will help:

- **Almond Flour:** Almond flour is more of an all-purpose flour and only contains 3 grams of carbs for 1/4 of a cup. (In comparison, totals are overwhelming for the regular wheat flour at 24 grams. This is why it is not on your diet plan!) almonds are blanched in boiling water to remove the skins and then ground into a fine flour used for baking low-carb cakes, cookies and pie crusts.

- **Almond Meal**: Almond meal isn't the same as almond flour. If you are running low on almond flour for baked goods like muffins and cookies, then merely throw some almonds in a food processor to make some almond meal.

- **Coconut Flour:** Each 1/4 cup of coconut flour contains 19 g of carbohydrates, 6 g of protein, 60 calories, 2.5 g of fat, 12 g of fiber, and 7 g of net carbs. It displays that tropical taste. Be sure it's stored in a closed container. Choose a spot where it's dark such as the pantry. The refrigerator and freezer could cause moisture contamination.

- **Ground Psyllium Husk Powder:** You will find this in several recipes. It is a binding agent with tons of fiber.

Low-Carb Sweeteners: Consider these choices:

- **Stevia Drops** include hazelnut, vanilla, English toffee, and chocolate flavors. Enjoy making a satisfying cup of sweetened coffee or other favorite drink. Some individuals think the drops are too bitter. At first, use only three drops to equal one teaspoon of sugar.

- **Swerve Granular Sweetener** is also an excellent choice as a blend. It's made from non-digestible carbs sourced from starchy root veggies and select fruits. Give it a try if you don't like the taste of stevia. Start with 3/4 of a teaspoon for every one of sugar. Increase the portion to your liking. Swerve also has its own confectioners or powdered sugar for your baking needs. On the downside, it is more expensive. You have to decide if it's worth the difference.

- **Xylitol** is at the top of the sugary list. It tastes just like sugar! The natural occurring sugar alcohol has the Glycemic index (GI) standing of 13. If you have tried others and weren't satisfied, this might be for you. Xylitol is also known to keep mouth bacteria in check which goes a long way to protect your dental health. The ingredient is commonly found in chewing gum. Unfortunately, if used in large amounts, it can cause diarrhea – making chewing gum a laxative if used in large quantities. *Pet Warning*: If you have a puppy in the house, be sure to use caution since it is toxic to dogs (even small amounts).

Chocolate: Dark chocolate is the best type for your Ketogenic diet. Sugar-free and the darker it is – the better. It is used in many of the following recipes.

Your Basic Shopping List

Take extra time to get organized before you begin your new diet plan. The items included in this segment will provide an excellent base stock for your menu planning needs. Store and clearly mark all food items that are used at the time the dessert is planned. All you need to do is count the carbs to remain in Ketosis. Each of the categories provides you with examples of the stock:

Pantry Items

These are some of the favorites for your baking and preparation of desserts while on the Ketogenic diet:

- Coconut flour
- Stevia
- Sugar-free gelatin
- Unsweetened cocoa powder
- Natural nut butter – no sugar

Dairy Products

It is essential to maintain your health using dairy products. It is best to choose fresh organic milk products. You can also add additional protein and calcium using non-dairy products such as cashew or almond milk. Keep these in the fridge:

- Heavy cream
- Butter
- Cream cheese
- Sour cream
- Ghee
- Parmesan cheese
- Sharp cheddar cheese

Healthy Fats

To achieve success in the Ketogenic diet, you need fats. These are some of those:

- Avocado
- Extra-virgin olive oil (EVOO)
- Sesame, avocado, and coconut oil

- Flaxseed oil
- Coconut flakes
- Olives

The Foods to *Avoid*

There are many healthy options to choose from while on the Ketogenic diet. Avoid the foods in the following groups – unless they are structured within this cookbook or other professional sources you trust. Each dessert item has been calculated with all of the nutritional information and servings listed.

- **Regular Dairy Milk**: Avoid regular milk for sure since it packs almost 13 grams of carbohydrates per cup.

- **Added Sugars**: The sugars to avoid include honey, maltose, dextrose, corn syrup, and maltodextrin.

- **Artificial Sweeteners**: Several types to avoid include saccharin, sucralose, and Splenda.

Benefits of MCT Oils

Your Ketogenic experience can improve with the use of MCT oil or medium chain triglycerides. These unique fatty acids are found in a natural form in palm and coconut oil. You will notice some of the smoothies use this as a component. These are just a few of the examples:

- The oil helps lower your blood sugar.
- The use of MCTs makes it much easier to get into – and remain – in Ketosis.
- It is a natural anti-convulsive.
- It is also excellent for appetite control and weight loss.

Important Note: Seek your doctor's advice before changing your eating patterns. In some cases, you could reduce the need for some medications.

Tools & Equipment

Each of these tools will help you speed up the baking process with your chosen dessert items.

Tool 1: Scales: It is almost a necessity to own a set of food scales to take out the guesswork. Keep this information in mind before you make the purchase:

- Seek a Conversion Button: You need to know how to convert measurements into grams since not all recipes have them listed. The grams keep the system in complete harmony.

- The Tare Function: When you set a bowl on the scale, the feature will allow you to reset the scale back to zero (0).

- Removable Plate: Keep the germs off the scale by removing the plate. Be sure it will come off to eliminate the bacterial buildup.

Tool 2: Food Processor, Immersion Blender or Regular Blender: Each of these will be an essential part of preparing many of the recipes for desserts.

Tool 3: Slow Cooker or Crockpot: You will find the crockpot a must if you have a busy lifestyle. These are just a couple of ways you can benefit from its use:

- Save a lot of Effort and Time: All it takes is a few good recipes and a little bit of your valuable time. In most of the cases, these recipes are geared towards a fast lifestyle and will be ready with just a few simple steps. After some time and practice, you will know which ones will be your favorites.

- Get Ahead of the Meal: Preparing food with your slow cooker can put you ahead of the game. You can prepare the cooker the night before if you have a busy day planned. All it takes is a few minutes of preparation. Just add all of the fixings into the pot and place it in the fridge – overnight. The next morning, transfer to the counter to become room temperature. Turn it on as you head out of the door and your dessert will be ready when you get home.

Tool 4: **Accurate Measuring Tools**: A measuring cup and spoon system that shows both the Metric and US standards of weight is essential, so there is no confusion during prep.

A Final Note: Some recipes might not be 100 % Keto-friendly. You can also adjust the ingredients to your own discretion. Remember this Formula: Total Carbs minus (-) Fiber = Net Carbs.

Chapter 2: Puddings, Scrumptious Candy, and Fat Bombs

Puddings

Nothing is handier for a treat than an individual fat bomb or a delicious candy choice. If you want something for a mid-morning choice, just try one of these healthy puddings.

Almond Blackberry Chia Pudding

Servings: 2
Macros: 1 g Net Carbs | 2 g Prot. | 8 g Fat | 109 Cal.

Ingredients:

- Fresh blackberries – 6 oz.
- Chia seeds – .25 cup
- Raw honey – 1 drizzle to taste
- Vanilla almond milk – 1.5 cups
- Sliced almonds – 2-3 tbsp.

Preparation Method:

1. Toss the berries into a dish, and crush with a fork until creamy.
2. Fold in a drizzle of honey, milk, and chia seeds. Stir well.
3. Refrigerate for several hours or overnight for best results.
4. Sprinkle with the almonds and several blackberries.
5. Serve and enjoy anytime.

Almond Pumpkin Pudding

Servings: 10
Macros: 4 g Net Carbs | 6 g Prot. | 16 g Fat | 154 Cal.

Ingredients:

- Coconut oil – 5 oz.
- Pumpkin puree – 10 oz.
- Coconut cream – 5 oz.
- Pumpkin pie spice – 1 tbsp.
- Powdered Erythritol – 3 tbsp.
- Almonds – 4 oz.
- Ginger – .75 tsp.

Preparation Method:

1. Combine and stir all of the fixings (omit the almonds) in a saucepan using the medium heat setting (10 min.).
2. Pour into silicone molds and press an almond inside each one.
3. Freeze for a minimum of one hour. Then you can remove from the molds and serve or freeze for later.
4. For a taste change, just squeeze a little lemon juice over the pudding before serving.

Cheesecake Pudding

Servings: 6 if you add berries or 4 without
Macros: 5 g Net Carbs | 5 g Prot. | 36 g Fat | 356 Cal.

Ingredients:

- Cream cheese or Neufchatel cheese – 1 block
- Heavy whipping cream – .5 cup
- Lemon juice – 1 tsp.
- Sour cream – .5 cup
- Liquid stevia – 20 drops
- Vanilla extract – 1 tsp.

Preparation Method:

1. Microwave the cream cheese for 30 seconds or leave on the counter to soften for a few minutes before using.
2. Whip the sour cream and whipping cream together with a hand mixer until soft peaks form. Combine with the rest of the fixings and whip until fluffy.
3. Portion into four dishes to chill. Cover with plastic wrap in the fridge.
4. When ready to eat, garnish with some berries if you like.
5. Please remember; if you add the berries, add the carbs.

Chocolate Avocado Pudding

Servings: 2
Macros: 2 g Net Carbs | 27 g Fat | 8 g Prot. | 281 Cal.

Ingredients:

- Room temperature cream cheese – 2 oz.
- Ripe medium avocado – 1
- Natural sweetener – swerve – 1 tsp.
- Vanilla extract – .25 tsp.
- Unsweetened cocoa powder – 4 tbsp.
- Pink salt – 1 pinch

Preparation Method:

1. Combine the cream cheese with the avocado, sweetener, vanilla, cocoa powder, and salt. Add to a blender or processor.
2. Pulse until creamy smooth.
3. Measure into a fancy dessert dishes and chill for at least 30 minutes.

Chocolate Hazelnut Avocado Mousse

Servings: 4
Macros: 4.6 g Net Carbs | 5.5 g Prot. | 25.6 g Fat | 280 Cal.

Ingredients:

- Avocados 14.1 oz – 1 Large
- Raw cacao powder or Dutch-process cocoa powder – 4 tbsp.
- Hazelnut butter – 4 tbsp.
- Sugar-free vanilla extract – .5 tsp.
- Powdered Swerve or Erythritol – 2 tbsp.
- Stevia extract – 10 drops
- Unsweetened almond milk/cashew milk/coconut milk – 4 tbsp. or 2 fl. Oz.
- Optional Topping: Chopped dark chocolate & Roasted chopped hazelnuts
- Also Needed: 4-single serving mason jars (5 oz. ea.).

Preparation Method:

1. Combine each of the fixings into a food processor (omit the milk).
2. Blend well, then, add the milk slowly until it's like you prefer.
3. Portion into the jars. Chill in the refrigerator for at least 15 minutes.
4. They will be good for up to 3 days if covered in an air-tight container the refrigerator.

Chocolate Mousse

Servings: 2
Macros: 4 g Net Carbs | 4 g Prot. | 50 g Fat | 460 Cal.

Ingredients:

- Heavy whipping cream – 1.5 tbsp.
- Swerve or another natural sweetener – 1 tbsp.
- Unsweetened cocoa powder – 1 tbsp.
- Butter – 4 tbsp.
- Cream Cheese – 4 tbsp.

Preparation Method:

1. Take the cream cheese and butter out of the refrigerator to become room temperature. Chill a bowl and whisk the cream. Store in the fridge.
2. In another dish, use a hand mixer to combine the sweetener, cream cheese, cocoa powder, and butter until well mixed.
3. Take out the refrigerated cream and fold into the chocolate mixture using a rubber scraper.
4. Portion into two dessert dishes and chill for one hour.

Cinnamon Roll Mousse

Servings: 4
Macros: 5.1 g Net Carbs | 29.3 g Fat | 4.6 g Prot. | 291 Cal.

Ingredients:

- Heavy whipping cream – .5 cup
- Softened full-fat cream cheese – 4.2 oz.
- Powdered Swerve or Erythritol – .25 cup
- Unsalted cashew butter or almond butter – 2 tbsp.
- Cinnamon – 1 tsp.
- Sugar-free vanilla extract – .5 tsp

Ingredients for the Drizzle:

- Coconut butter – 2 tbsp.
- Swerve or Erythritol – 1 tbsp.
- Virgin coconut oil – 1 tsp.
- Also Needed: 4 mason jars

Preparation Method:

1. Combine the heavy cream and cream cheese until smooth. Toss in the rest of the fixings (sweetener to taste).
2. In another container, combine the drizzle components and place in the microwave. Using 10-second intervals, warm it up until it is syrupy.
3. Portion the mouse in the jars and drizzle with the syrup. Dust with some cinnamon and enjoy! It's good for up to five days in the fridge.

Keto Chia Pudding

Servings: 4
Macros: 12 g Net Carbs | 5 g Prot. | 24 g Fat | 273 Cal.

Ingredients:

- Whole ripe avocado – 1
- Chia seeds – .25 cup
- Medium dates – 2
- Almond or coconut milk – 1 cup
- Vanilla extract – .5 tsp.

Preparation Method:

1. Pour the milk, vanilla, avocado, and dates into a blender.
2. Blend until well mixed. Empty over the chia seeds and cover overnight in the refrigerator when you go to bed. You can also let it rest for two to four hours before serving.

Lemon Custard – Slow Cooker

Servings: 4
Macros: 3 g Net Carbs | 7 g Prot. | 30 g Fat | 319 Cal.

Ingredients:

- Fresh lemon juice – .25 cup
- Large egg yolks – 5
- Lemon zest – 1 tbsp.
- Liquid stevia – .5 tsp.
- Vanilla extract – 1 tsp.
- Coconut cream/whipping cream – 2 cups
- Optional: Whipped coconut cream
- Also Needed: Ramekins/4 small jars

Preparation Method:

1. Whisk the liquid stevia, egg yolks, lemon juice, lemon zest, and vanilla. Whip in the heavy cream. Divide into the four jars.
2. Add a rack in the cooker and arrange the jars on top of it. Add water to fill half of the way up the sides of the ramekins.
3. Secure the lid and cook three hours on low.
4. Transfer the jars from the cooker and cool to room temperature. Chill in the fridge approximately three hours.
5. Serve with the whipped cream if desired.

Pumpkin Custard – Crockpot

Servings: 6
Macros: 3 g Net Carbs | 5 g Prot. | 12 g Fat | 147 Cal.

Ingredients:

- Large eggs – 4
- Granulated stevia/Erythritol blend – .5 cup
- Sea salt – .125 tsp.
- Vanilla extract – 1 tsp.
- Pumpkin pie spice – 1 tsp.
- Butter/coconut oil/ghee – 4 tbsp.
- Pumpkin puree Canned or homemade – 1 tsp.
- Super-fine almond flour – .5 cup
- Recommended Size for the Cooker: 3-4-quarts
- Coconut cooking oil spray or butter for the pot

Preparation Method:

1. Take the butter out of the refrigerator to become room temperature. Lightly grease or spray the cooker.
2. Use a mixer to whisk the eggs – blending until smooth. Slowly, add the sweetener.
3. Blend in the vanilla extract and puree. Fold in the pie spice, salt, and almond flour. Mix everything well and add to the crockpot.
4. Secure the lid – with a paper towel between the top and the fixings to absorb moisture on top of the custard.
5. Cook for 2 to 2.75 hours on the low setting. When it's done, it will begin to pull away from the slow cooker. The center will be set.
6. Enjoy warm and top it off with garnishes as desired.

Candy

Chocolate Bonbons

Servings: 6
Macros: -0- g Net Carbs | 1 g Prot. | 10 g Fat | 100 Cal.

Ingredients:

- Butter – 5 tbsp.
- Coconut oil – 3 tbsp.
- Sugar-free raspberry syrup – 2 tbsp.
- Cocoa powder – 2 tbsp.

Preparation Method:

1. Mix the entire batch of ingredients in a pan.
2. Empty the bombs into six molds or muffin tins.
3. Place the prepared tin into the freezer for a minimum of two hours. Enjoy!

Chocolate Coconut Bites

Servings: 6
Macros: 9 g Net Carbs | 9 g Prot. | 27 g Fat | 326 Cal.

Ingredients:

- Unsweetened 80% or higher dark chocolate – 4 oz.
- Heavy cream – .33 cup
- Coconut flour – 1 cup
- Chocolate protein powder – 1 tbsp.
- Shredded unsweetened coconut – .25 cup
- Coconut oil – 4 tbsp.

Preparation Method:

1. Dice the dark chocolate into bits.
2. Warm up the heavy cream in a saucepan (med-low). Stir in the chocolate bits and oil. Continue stirring until combined and remove from the burner.
3. Stir in the protein powder and coconut flour. Store in the refrigerator for a minimum of two hours.
4. Take the dough out of the fridge when they are cool. Shape into balls and roll through the shredded coconut until coated.
5. Store in the fridge in a closed container.

Chocolate Covered Almonds

Servings: 1
Macros: 3 g Net Carbs | 4 g Prot. | 15 g Fat | 183 Cal.

Ingredients:

- Unsweetened dark chocolate baking chips – .75 cup
- Whole raw almonds – 1.5 cups
- Pure vanilla extract – 1 tsp.
- Sea salt – 1 pinch

Preparation Method:

1. Cut a piece of parchment paper and cover a baking tray.
2. Toss the chips into a saucepan using low heat. Stir and add the vanilla.
3. Once the chocolate is melted, add the almonds and stir until coated.
4. Arrange them on the baking tin and dust with the salt.
5. Place in the fridge for a minimum of 30 minutes before you are ready to devour your portion.
6. For a taste change, sprinkle with some ground cinnamon.

Coconut Peanut Butter Balls

Servings: 15
Macros: 0.92 g Net Carbs | 0.98 g Prot. | 3.19 g Fat | 35.1 Cal.

Ingredients:

- Creamy peanut butter – Keto-friendly – 3 tbsp.
- Powdered Erythritol – 2.5 tsp.
- Unsweetened cocoa powder – 3 tsp.
- Almond flour – 2 tsp.
- Unsweetened coconut flakes – .5 cup

Preparation Method:

1. Combine the peanut butter, Erythritol, cocoa, and flour. Place in the freezer for one hour.
2. Spoon out a small spoon size of the butter mix. Roll into the flakes until it is covered.
3. Refrigerate overnight for the best results and enjoy.

Cream Cheese Truffles – Party Time

Servings: 24
Macros: 1.67 g Net Carbs | 1.23 g Prot. | 7 g Fat | 72.7 Cal.

Ingredients:

- Cream cheese, softened – 16 oz.
- Unsweetened cocoa powder – divided – .5 cup
- Swerve confectioners – 4 tbsp.
- Liquid Stevia – .25 tsp.
- Rum extract – .5 tsp.
- Instant coffee – 1 tbsp.
- Water – 2 tbsp.
- Heavy whipping cream – 1 tbsp.
- Paper candy cups for serving – 24

Preparation Method:

1. Combine all of the fixings (set aside 1/4 cup of cocoa powder). Blend well with a hand mixer. Chill in the fridge for about 30 minutes.
2. Dust the countertop with the rest of the cocoa powder. Roll out heaping tablespoons of the mixture in your hands to form about 24 balls.
3. Roll the balls through the powder and place into individual candy cups.
4. Chill for another hour before serving.

Crust-less Cheesecake Bites

Servings: 4
Macros: 2 g Net Carbs | 5 g Prot. | 15 g Fat | 169 Cal.

Ingredients:

- Large eggs – 2
- Sour cream – .25 cup
- Vanilla extract – .25 tsp.
- Room temperature cream cheese – 4 oz.
- Natural sweetener – ex. swerve – .33 cup

Preparation Method:

1. Warm up the oven to reach 350°F. Use a hand mixer to combine the ingredients.
2. Prepare a cupcake pan with 4 disposable paper cups or silicone liners.
3. Fill the cups and bake for 30 minutes.
4. After cooling about 3 hours, serve and enjoy.
5. You can save the extras for up to 3 months if stored in zip-lock type bags.

Macaroons

Servings: 1
Macros: 4 g Net Carbs | 2 g Prot. | 10 g Fat | 90 Cal.

Ingredients:

- Egg whites – 4
- Vanilla – 1 tsp.
- Artificial sweetener of choice – 1 cup
- Water – 4.5 tsp.
- Unsweetened coconut – .5 cup

Preparation Method:

1. Warm up the oven to 325°F.
2. Whisk the eggs with the liquid components. Stir in the coconut and mix.
   Use an immersion blender for uniform consistency.
3. Add the batter into the greased pan and bake for 15 minutes. Enjoy!

No-Bake Chocolate Fudge Haystacks

Servings: 12
Macros: 1.5 g Net Carbs | 2 g Prot. | 18 g Fat | 172 Cal.

Ingredients:

- Softened cream cheese – 4 oz.
- Erythritol sweetener – .75 cup
- Softened unsalted butter – .5 cup
- Unsweetened cocoa powder – .25 cup
- Coarse sea salt – .125 tsp.
- Unsweetened desiccated/shredded coconut – 1 cup
- Sugar-free vanilla extract – 1 tsp.
- Chopped walnuts – .33 cups

Preparation Method:

1. Blend the cocoa powder, sweetener, cheese, and butter using a fork or mixer. Stir in the walnuts, coconut, salt, and vanilla extract.
2. Scoop out one-inch balls to make haystacks. Chill approximately 30 minutes or longer.

Peanut Butter & Chocolate Cups

Servings: 12
Macros: 2.2 g Net Carbs | 3.4 g Prot. | 26 g Fat | 246 Cal.

Ingredients:

- Coconut oil – 1 cup
- Heavy cream – 2 tbsp.
- Natural peanut butter or another butter – .5 cup
- Cocoa powder – 1 tbsp.
- Kosher salt – .25 tsp.
- Vanilla extract – .25 tsp.
- Roasted chopped salted peanuts or another nut – 1 oz.

Preparation Method:

1. Use the low setting on the stovetop to prepare a saucepan with the coconut oil. Once it's hot (3-5 min.), stir in the rest of the fixings.
2. Pour into the silicone muffin molds or use an ice tray. Sprinkle with the nuts and put them on a baking tray.
3. Freeze until it's firm for about one hour. Pop out of the molds and place in an airtight container to enjoy.

Pecan Turtle Truffles

Servings: 15
Macros: 1 g Net Carbs | 14 g Fat | 4 g Prot. | 142 Cal.

Ingredients:

- Swerve for your preference – .33 cup
- Melted butter – .5 cup
- Vanilla extract – .25 tsp.
- Caramel extract – .5 tsp.
- Vanilla protein powder -0- carbs – .33 cup
- Finely ground pecans – 1 cup
- Lindt or your choice – 85% chocolate – 4 squares
- Pecan halves – 15

Preparation Method:

1. Combine the sweetener, butter, vanilla extract, caramel extracts, finely ground pecans and protein powder in a mixing container.
2. Roll into 15 truffles and place on a sheet of parchment or waxed paper.
3. Melt the chocolate in a baggie in the microwave for one minute. Snip the corner and squeeze the chocolate over the prepared truffles.
4. Garnish each truffle with a pecan half. Chill and enjoy any time.

Raspberry Fudge

Servings: 12
Macros: 4.4 g Net Carbs | 2.6 g Prot. | 25.3 g Fat | 242 Cal.

Ingredients:

- Cream cheese – 16 oz.
- Butter – 1 cup
- White sugar substitute – .25 cup
- Unsweetened cocoa powder – 6 tbsp.
- Heavy cream – 2 tbsp.
- Raspberry extract – 1 tsp.
- Vanilla extract – 2 tsp.
- Chopped walnuts – .33 cup

Preparation Method:

1. Take the cream cheese and butter out of the fridge ahead of time until it reaches room temperature. Next, combine the cream cheese and butter in a large microwavable container using an electric mixer. When smooth, mix with the rest of the fixings until well incorporated.
2. Microwave using the high setting for 30 seconds. Blend with the mixer again until smooth.
3. Empty into the prepared pan (1-inch layer). Cover and chill for at least 2 hours in the fridge.
4. Slice into 12 portions. Serve and enjoy or store for a delicious treat later.

Slow Cooked Sugar-Free Fudge

Servings: 30
Macros: 2 g Net Carbs | 1 g Prot. | 5 g Fat | 65 Cal.

Ingredients:

- Sugar-free chocolate chips – 2.5 cups
- Coconut milk – .33 cup
- Salt – 1 pinch or so
- Pure vanilla extract – 1 tsp.
- Vanilla liquid stevia – optional – 2 tsp.
- Suggested: 3-4 quart-size

Preparation Method:

1. Mix all of the goodies in the cooker. Close the lid and cook for two hours on the low setting.
2. Take the lid off and unplug the unit. Don't stir for 30 minutes to one hour. Lastly, mix for five minutes until creamy smooth.
3. Line a one-quart dish with some parchment paper. Spread the fudge into the plate, and chill until firm.

Walnut Fudge

Servings: 12
Macros: 1.1 g Net Carbs | 1.8 g Prot. | 14.1 g Fat | 134 Cal.

Ingredients:

- Cream cheese – 4 oz.
- Butter – 1 stick (+) 1 tbsp.
- Granulated sweetener 2 tbsp. or to taste
- Vanilla – 1 tsp.
- Dark cocoa powder – 3 tbsp.
- Walnut pieces – .33 cup

Preparation Method:

1. Let the cream cheese and butter warm up to room temperature and combine. Mix well until the lumps are gone.
2. Stir in the sweetener, cocoa, and vanilla. Combine well and add the nuts.
3. Add to a lined plate and store in the fridge to set. Slice and enjoy.

White Chocolate Bark

Servings: 12
Macros: -0- g Net Carbs | -0- g Prot. | 2 g Fat | 40 Cal.

Ingredients:

- Cocoa butter – .25 cup
- Low-carb sweetener – .33 cup
- Vanilla powder – 1 tsp.
- Hemp seed powder – .5 tsp.
- Toasted pumpkin seeds – 1 tsp.
- Salt
- Coconut oil – for the bowl

Preparation Method:

1. Chop the cocoa butter into fine bits. Add water to a double boiler and add the pieces to melt using the medium heat setting. Stir in the rest of the fixings.
2. Lightly grease a bowl using a spritz of oil and add the mixture.
3. Let it cool and break into 12 portions.

White Chocolate Pecan Halves

Servings: 10
Macros: 1.4 g Net Carbs | 2 g Prot. | 8.9 g Fat | 123 Cal.

Ingredients:

- Pecan halves – 10 oz.
- Caramel sugar-free candies – 10
- Cocoa butter – 2 oz.
- Erythritol – 3 tbsp.
- Cinnamon – dash

Preparation Method:

1. Warm up the oven to 300°F.
2. Place a piece of the caramel candy on top of each of the pecan halves. Bake until they are slightly melted.
3. In a saucepan, combine the Erythritol, cocoa butter, and cinnamon until creamy. Spoon over each of the nuts and chill in the refrigerator for two hours.
4. When ready, just enjoy!

Delicious Fat Bombs

Allspice Almond Fat Bombs

Servings: 8
Macros: 2 g Net Carbs | 5 g Prot. | 22 g Fat | 214 Cal.

Ingredients:

- Heavy cream – 5 tbsp.
- Almond butter – 10 tbsp.
- Coconut oil – 4 tbsp.
- Allspice – .25 tsp.
- Cocoa powder – 2 tsp.
- Liquid stevia – 6 drops
- Chopped almonds – optional

Preparation Method:

1. Mix the top six ingredients, and add the almonds (if using). Transfer the bombs into a mold or other container.
2. Freeze for approximately two hours. Top with chopped almonds.
3. Remove and enjoy.

Almond Butter Fat Bombs

Servings: 8
Macros: 1.7 g Net Carbs | 1.5 g Prot. | 14.7 g Fat | 145 Cal.

Ingredients:

- Almond butter – 9.5 tbsp.
- Melted coconut oil – .75 cup
- Liquid stevia – .25 tsp. or to your taste
- Melted salted butter – 9 tbsp.
- Cocoa – 3 tbsp.

Preparation Method:

1. Combine all of the components listed until smooth.
2. Add the final product to 24 mini muffin molds or use silicone candy molds.
3. Freeze for a minimum of 30 minutes. Pop them out and enjoy.

Almond – Choco Fat Bombs

Servings: 24
Macros: -0- g Net Carbs | 0.5 g Prot. | 9.6 g Fat | 75 Cal.

Ingredients:

- Cocoa powder – unsweetened – 3 tbsp.
- Organic coconut oil – 1 cup
- Sweetener – 3-4 tbsp.
- Almond butter – 1 cup
- Optional: Splash almond extract

Preparation Method:

1. On the stovetop using medium heat, warm up a pan. Melt the coconut oil and almond butter. Blend in the sweetener of your choice with the cocoa powder.
2. Take the pan off of the heat to add the almond extract. Empty the contents into a silicone candy mold.
3. Refrigerate/freeze until set.
4. Store the goodies in an airtight container in the refrigerator.

Blackberry Coconut Fat Bombs

Servings: 16
Macros: 3 g Net Carbs | 1.1 g Prot. | 18.7 g Fat | 170 Cal.

Ingredients:

- Coconut butter – 1 cup
- Coconut oil – 1 cup
- Fresh or frozen blackberries – .5 cup
- Vanilla extract – .5 tsp.
- Stevia drops – add more for a sweeter taste
- Lemon juice – 1 tbsp.
- Also Needed: 6x6 container

Preparation Method:

1. Add the coconut oil, coconut butter, and frozen berries in a cooking pot using the medium heat setting. Line a baking pan with a sheet of parchment paper.
2. Use a small blender or food processor and add the mixture (step1) along with the rest of the components in the recipe. Spread it out on the prepared pan. Chill in the refrigerator for at least one hour.
3. *Note*: If you use fresh berries you won't need to cook them with the butter and coconut oil (step 1).

Blueberry Cream Cheese Fat Bombs

Servings: 12
Macros: 0.99 g Net Carbs | 0.96 g Prot. | 7.4 g Fat | 67 Cal.

Ingredients:

- Cream cheese – 1.5 cups
- Fresh or frozen berries – 1 cup
- Swerve – 2-3 tbsp.
- Vanilla extract – 1 tbsp.
- Coconut oil – .5 cup

Preparation Method:

1. For 30 to 60 minutes before preparation time, place the cream cheese on the countertop to become room temperature.
2. Take the stems off the berries and rinse. Pour into a blender. Mix well until smooth.
3. Pour in the Swerve and extract. Blend in the oil and cream cheese.
4. Add the mixture to candy molds and freeze for approximately two hours until set.

Bulletproof Fat Bombs

Servings: 20
Macros: 0.5 g Net Carbs | 0.8 g Prot. | 8.1 g Fat | 77 Cal.

Ingredients:

- Creamed coconut milk/full-fat cream cheese – 1 cup
- Butter – .25 cup
- Raw unsweetened cocoa powder – 2 tbsp.
- MCT oil/or more coconut oil – 2 tbsp.
- Swerve/Erythritol – .25 cup
- Liquid Stevia extract – 10-15 drops
- Strong brewed coffee – room-temperature – .5 cup
- Rum extract – optional – 1 tsp.

Preparation Method:

1. Combine the creamed milk and butter along with the cocoa powder, and stevia into a blender. Pulse until creamy smooth.
2. Pour in the coffee, pulse, and pour into an ice cream maker. Wait for approximately 30 to 60 minutes. The times will depend upon the type of maker used.
3. Empty the bombs into small muffin tins using about 2 tablespoons for each bomb. Let them cool for two to three hours in the freezer until firmed up.
4. *Note:* You can substitute 1-2 teaspoons of instant coffee powder and not need an ice-cream maker. You could also use a regular blender.

Cacao Coconut Fat Bombs

Servings: 12
Macros: 0.9 g Net Carbs | 0.7 g Prot. | 10.6 g Fat | 96 Cal.

Ingredients:

- Raw cacao powder – 1 tbsp.
- Liquid vanilla stevia – 5-10 drops
- Melted coconut oil – .5 cup
- Chopped almonds – optional – .25 cup
- Sea salt – a pinch – optional

Preparation Method:

1. Mix the cacao powder, stevia, and coconut oil.
2. Empty the mixture into parchment-lined muffin tins or a dish.
3. Put it in the fridge for at least one hour until firm. Pop the bombs out or cut into 12 portions.
4. Storage: Freezer for several months or the fridge for one week.

Chocolate Fat Bombs

Servings: 24
Macros: 1 g Net Carbs | 3 g Prot. | 21 g Fat | 180 Cal.

Ingredients:

- Coconut oil – .5 cup
- Splenda or your preference – 3 packets
- Walnut or almond butter – .25 cup
- Sugar-free coffee liqueur syrup – ex. Da Vinci – 2 tbsp.
- Heavy whipping cream – .25 cup
- Walnut halves – 24
- Also Needed: Silicon molds

Preparation Method:

1. Use a glass measuring cup and add the oil, walnut butter, coffee liqueur, cocoa powder, and sweetener.
2. Microwave 30-40 seconds. Stir the contents until the oil melts.
3. Stir in the cream and pour into the molds. Arrange a nut in each one and freeze until set.

Chocolate Peanut Butter Fat Bombs

Servings: 12
Macros: 1.1 Net Carbs | 1.7 g Prot. | 8.7 g Fat | 88 Cal.

Ingredients:

- Coconut oil – .25 cup
- Sugar-free peanut butter – .25 cup
- Unsweetened baking chocolate – 1 oz.
- Cocoa – 1 tbsp.
- Stevia drops – vanilla – .5 tsp.

Preparation Method:

1. Use a double boiler and melt the oil, peanut butter, cocoa, and baking chocolate.
2. Remove from the burner and add the stevia. Pour into the molds and freeze. When hard, store a closed plastic bowl in the freezer.

Chocolate Peppermint Fat Bombs

Servings: 6
Macros: 1.1 g Net Carbs | 0.4 g Prot. | 21 g Fat | 188 Cal.

Ingredients:

- Granulated sweetener – your choice – 1 tbsp.
- Melted coconut – 4.5 oz.
- Unsweetened coconut – 2 tbsp.
- Peppermint essence – .25 tsp.

Preparation Method:

1. Combine the sweetener, coconut oil, and peppermint essence.
2. Pour about half of the bomb into six ice cube trays. Let them stay in the fridge for a layer of white.
3. Use the remainder of the mixture to blend in with the cocoa powder.
4. Empty the chocolate mix on top of the trays.
5. Sit it back into the fridge until firm. Then, pop out and enjoy.

Coconut Macaroons Fat Bombs

Servings: 10
Macros: 0.5 g Net Carbs | 1.8 g Prot. | 5 g Fat | 46 Cal.

Ingredients:

- Shredded coconut – .5 cup
- Organic almond flour – .25 cup
- Swerve – 2 tbsp.
- Coconut oil – 1 tbsp.
- Vanilla extract – 1 tbsp.
- Egg whites – 3

Preparation Method:

1. In a mixing bowl, blend the swerve, coconut, and almond flour until well combined.
2. Warm the oil in a saucepan and stir in the vanilla.
3. Place a medium-sized bowl in the freezer.
4. Combine the oil into the flour mixture, mixing well.
5. Put the whites of the eggs into the cold dish and whisk until stiff – foamy peaks are formed. Fold in the whites with the flour.
6. Scoop the mixture into the baking sheet/muffin cups.
7. Bake until the macaroons are lightly browned or about eight minutes.
8. Cool before placing on a serving dish.

Coffee Fat Bombs

Servings: 15
Macros: -0- g Net Carbs | 4 g Fat | -0- g Prot. | 45 Cal.

Ingredients:

- Cream cheese – room temperature – 4.4 oz.
- Powdered Xylitol – 2 tbsp.
- Instant coffee – 1 tbsp.
- Coconut oil – 1 tbsp.
- Unsweetened cocoa powder – 1 tbsp.
- Room temperature butter – 1 tbsp.

Instructions:

1. Take the butter and cream cheese out of the fridge about an hour before it's time to begin.
2. With a blender/food processor, blitz the xylitol and coffee into a fine powder. Add the hot water to form a pasty mix.
3. Blend in the butter, cream cheese, cocoa powder, and coconut oil.
4. Add to ice cube trays and freeze a minimum of one to two hours.
5. Use Ziploc bags to keep them fresh in the freezer.

Coffee Fat Bombs

Servings: 15
Macros: -0- g Net Carbs | -0- g Prot. | 4 g Fat | 45 Cal.

Ingredients:

- Cream cheese – room temperature – 4.4 oz.
- Powdered xylitol – 2 tbsp.
- Instant coffee – 1 tbsp.
- Room temperature butter – 1 tbsp.
- Coconut oil – 1 tbsp.
- Unsweetened cocoa powder – 1 tbsp.

Preparation Method:

1. With a blender/food processor, blitz the xylitol and coffee into a fine powder. Add the hot water to form a pasty mix.
2. Blend in the butter, cream cheese, cocoa powder, and coconut oil.
3. Add to ice cube trays and freeze a minimum of one to two hours.
4. Use Ziploc bags to keep them fresh in the freezer.

Craving Buster Fat Bombs

Servings: 32
Macros: 2.25 g Net Carbs | 1.75 g Prot. | 22.5 g Fat | 122.5 Cal.

Ingredients:

- Organic cacao powder – 1 cup
- Melted organic coconut oil – 1 cup
- Almond butter – 1 cup
- Muffin tins – 32-count

Preparation Method:

1. Melt the oil and whisk in with the almond butter and cacao.
2. Spoon 1/2 tablespoon of the product into the 32 small paper muffin cups.
3. Freeze or refrigerate until hard and store in the fridge.
4. *Note:* If you want just one bomb; melt the oil and just add 1/2 tablespoon of each ingredient to enjoy.

Dark Chocolate Fat Bombs

Servings: 12
Macros: 5.6 g Net Carbs | 10.5 g Fat | 4 g Prot. | 96 Cal.

Ingredients:

- Stevia extract – 1 tsp.
- Butter/coconut oil – .5 cup
- Almond butter – .5 cup
- Dark chocolate – 85% or higher – 3 oz.
- Sea salt – .25 tsp.

Preparation Method:

1. With the use of a double boiler, combine all of the components in the recipe until smooth.
2. Empty the mixture into 12 ice trays and freeze for a minimum of one hour.
3. Serve or enjoy when the sugar urge strikes.

Dark Chocolate Raspberry Fat Bombs

Servings: 14
Macros: 2.6 g Net Carbs | 2.2 g Prot. | 17 g Fat | 164 Cal.

Ingredients:

- Extra-virgin coconut oil – 3 tbsp.
- Cocoa butter – .5 cup
- Unsweetened dark chocolate – 100% cacao – 4.2 oz.
- Unsweetened vanilla extract – 1 tsp. or 1 vanilla bean
- Unsweetened cacao powder – .33 cup
- Stevia extract – vanilla/clear/chocolate – 20-25 drops
- Swerve or Erythritol – powdered – 1/2 – 3/4 cup

Preparation Method:

1. Roast the almonds in a pan for five minutes.
2. Add an almond to each raspberry and freeze for one hour.
3. Using a dish over a pan of hot water or a double boiler, melt the unsweetened chocolate, coconut oil, and cocoa butter. Powder the Swerve for a smooth texture in a blender.
4. Remove the seeds from the bean (if using) by slicing the bean lengthwise and scraping out the seeds. Add them along with the unsweetened cacao, stevia, and powdered Erythritol.
5. Pour the mixture into papers with the use of a mini muffin tin, one tablespoon for each one. Add two loaded raspberries and pour one more tablespoon of the chocolate to cover.
6. Put the bombs in the freezer until set, for about 30 minutes.

Lemonade Fat Bombs

Servings: 2
Macros: 7 g Net Carbs | 4 g Prot. | 43 g Fat | 404 Cal.

Ingredients:

- Cream cheese – 4 oz.
- Butter – 2 oz.
- Lemon zest & juice – .5 of 1 lemon
- Swerve – 2 tsp.
- Pink Himalayan salt – 1 pinch or to taste

Preparation Method:

1. Take the butter and cream cheese out of the fridge and let it become room temperature before using. Zest the lemon and juice it into a small dish.
2. In another container, mix the butter with the cream cheese. Use a hand mixer to combine all of the fixings until well mixed.
3. Spoon the mixture into small molds or cupcake paper liners in a muffin tin pan.
4. Stick the chosen holder in the freezer for two hours. Take them out of the molds and put them in a zipper-top baggie to enjoy any time. Store in the freezer for up to three months.

Maple Almond Fudge Fat Bombs

Servings: 24
Macros: 1.5 g Net Carbs | 1 g Prot. | 6 g Fat | 58 Cal.

Ingredients:

- Coconut oil – 2 tbsp.
- Butter – .25 cup
- All-natural almond butter – .5 cup
- Sugar-free maple syrup – 1 tbsp.
- Also Needed: Mini muffin tin & paper liners

Preparation Method:

1. Melt the butter, almond butter, and coconut oil for two minutes in the microwave. Stir every 30 seconds until melted. Whisk in the syrup and stir.
2. Pour the fixings into the prepared tins. Place in the fridge until hardened. Dice into 24 bite-sized pieces.
3. You can also store in the freezer or at room temperature, depending on the desired consistency.

Pistachio & Almond Fat Bombs

Servings: 36
Macros: 3.1 g Net Carbs | 2.2 g Prot. | 17.4 g Fat | 170 Cal.

Ingredients:

- Roasted almond butter – 1 cup
- Firm coconut oil – 1 cup
- Creamy coconut butter – 1 cup
- Cacao butter – melted – .5 cup
- Full-fat coconut milk – .5 cup
- Chai spice – 2 tsp.
- Ghee – .25 cup
- Pure vanilla extract – 1 tbsp.
- Raw shelled pistachios – .25 tsp.
- Himalayan salt – .25 tsp.
- Pure almond extract – .25 tsp.
- Also Needed: 9-inch square baking pan

Preparation Method:

1. Chill the coconut milk overnight.
2. Grease the pan and line it with parchment paper.
3. Melt the butter in a saucepan or microwave and set aside.
4. Add everything except the pistachios and cacao butter in a large bowl. Use the slow speeds and increase using a hand mixer until it is airy and light.
5. Empty the melted cacao into the almond mix and continue mixing until it is well incorporated.
6. Add it to the prepared pan and sprinkle with the chopped pistachios.
7. Refrigerate at least four hours. It is much better if chilled overnight.
8. Cut into 36 squares and enjoy.

Raspberry Coconut Bark Fat Bombs

Servings: 12
Macros: 2.45 g Net Carbs | 1.7 g Prot. | 23.6 g Fat | 234 Cal.

Ingredients:

- Powdered swerve sweetener – .25 cup
- Freeze-dried raspberries – .5 cup
- Coconut oil – .5 cup
- Coconut butter – .5 cup
- Unsweetened shredded coconut – .5 cup
- Also Needed: 8 x 8 pan with parchment paper

Preparation Method:

1. Prepare the baking pan and grind the berries in a food processor or coffee grinder until they are powdery.
2. Using the medium heat setting, add the oil, butter, sweetener, and coconut in a small saucepan. Stir until combined.
3. Pour half of the mixture into the pan and add the raspberry mixture to the other half of the batter and stir.
4. Drop by the spoonful into the coconut base and swirl to make a pretty design. Refrigerate or freeze and break into chunks for a tasty snack.

Stuffed Pecan Fat Bombs

Servings: 1
Macros: 2 g Net Carbs | 11 g Prot. | 31 g Fat | 150 Cal.

Ingredients:

- Pecan halves – 4
- Neufchatel cheese/cream cheese – 1 oz.
- Coconut butter/unsalted butter – .5 tbsp.
- Sea salt – 1 pinch
- Your favorite flavor mix – herb or veggie

Preparation Method:

1. Warm up the oven to 350°F oven. Once it's hot, toast the pecans for 8 to 10 minutes. Let cool.
2. Allow the cream cheese and butter to soften. Add the mixture with your favorite flavor, veggie, or herb and mix until smooth.
3. Spread the tasty fixings between the two pecan halves.
4. Drizzle with some sea salt.

Chapter 3: Cookies Galore

You are sure to find the perfect cookie for any time of the day or night!

Amaretti Cookies

Servings: 16
Macros: 1 g Net Carbs | 2.5 g Prot. | 8 g Fat | 86 Cal.

Ingredients:

- Coconut flour – 2 tbsp.
- Almond flour – 1 cup
- Baking powder – .5 tsp.
- Cinnamon – .25 tsp.
- Salt – .5 tsp
- Erythritol – .5 cup
- Eggs – 2
- Coconut oil – 4 tbsp.
- Vanilla extract – .5 tsp
- Almond extract – .5 tsp
- Sugar-free jam – 2 tbsp.
- Shredded coconut – 1 tbsp.

Preparation Method:

1. Line a baking tin with parchment paper. Warm up the oven to reach 400°F. Combine all of the dry fixings. After combined, work in the wet ones.
2. Shape into 16 cookies. Make a dent in the center of each one. Bake for 15-17 minutes.
3. Let them cool a few minutes before adding a dab of jam to each one and a sprinkle of the coconut bits.

Chocolate Cookies

Servings: 16
Macros: 10 g Net Carbs | 17 g Prot. | 14 g Fat | 155 Cal.

Ingredients:

- Butter – 7 tbsp.
- Almond flour – 2 cups
- Granulated sweetener – .75 cup
- Dark chocolate – 2 oz.
- Eggs – 2
- Orange zest – 1 tbsp.
- Orange extract – 1 tsp.
- Vanilla extract – 1 tsp.
- Orange juice – 1 tbsp.
- Baking powder – .75 tsp.
- Baking soda – .5 tsp.
- Salt – .5 tsp.

Preparation Method:

1. Warm up the oven to reach 350°F.
2. Combine the dry fixings (baking soda, salt, flour, baking powder, and sweetener).
3. Use a microwavable dish to melt the butter and stir in the orange zest, juice, the orange extract, and vanilla extract.
4. Combine all of the fixings and mix well.
5. Add the dough onto a baking tin. Form into a rectangle and slice into 16 servings. Bake for 20-25 minutes.

Chocolate Chip Cookies

Servings: 24
Macros: 2 g Net Carbs | 2 g Prot. | 8 g Fat | 90 Cal.

Ingredients:

- Molasses – optional – .5 tsp.
- Large egg – 1
- Sweetener – swerve – .66 cup
- Cold – room temperature butter – 5.5 tbsp.
- Vanilla extract – .5 tsp.
- Almond flour – 1.25 cups
- Sea salt – optional – .125 tsp.
- Baking powder – 1.5 tsp.
- Coconut flour – 1 tbsp.
- Chopped pecans – optional – .25 cup
- Chocolate chips – sugar-free – .5 cup

Preparation Method:

1. Use some parchment paper or silicone baking mats to line two baking sheets. Set the oven temperature to 325°F. Use a mixer to blend the sweetener and butter. Mix in the molasses, egg, and vanilla extract until well combined.
2. In another container, combine the two flours, sea salt, and baking powder, stirring until blended.
3. Fold in the pecans and chocolate chips. Arrange the cookie dough by the tablespoonful into the prepared pans. They should be 1.5-inches apart.
   Bake until the bottoms are browned or about 12-15 minutes. Let them cool until firm and set (minimum 25 minutes).

Chocolate Coconut Cookies

Servings: 20
Macros: 1 g Net Carbs | 2.2 g Prot. | 6.8 g Fat | 77 Cal.

Ingredients:

- Almond flour – 1 cup
- Coconut flour – 3 tbsp.
- Salt – .25 tsp.
- Unsweetened shredded coconut – .33 cup
- Erythritol – .33 cup
- Baking powder – .5 tsp.
- Cocoa powder – .25 cup
- Coconut oil – .25 cup
- Vanilla extract – .25 tsp.
- Room-temperature eggs – 2

Preparation Method:

1. Warm up the oven to 350°F. Cover a baking tin with some parchment paper.
2. Combine the dry fixings and mix with a hand mixer.
3. In another dish, combine the wet components and add to the dry until well blended.
4. Break apart pieces of the cookie dough and roll into 20 balls.
5. Arrange on the cookie sheet and bake 15-20 minutes.

Chocolate-Filled Peanut Butter Cookies

Servings: 20
Macros: 2.7 g Net Carbs | 4.5 g Prot. | 14 g Fat | 150 Cal.

Ingredients:

- Almond flour – 2.5 cups
- Peanut butter – .5 cup
- Coconut oil – .25 cup
- Erythritol – .25 cup
- Maple syrup – 3 tbsp.
- Vanilla extract – 1 tbsp.
- Baking powder – 1.5 tsp.
- Salt – .5 tsp
- Dark chocolate bars – 2-3

Preparation Method:

1. Prepare a baking tin with a sheet of parchment paper.
2. Warm up the oven to reach 350°F.
3. Whisk each of the wet fixings together. Mix each of the dry ingredients. Sift them into the wet components. Mix well and place in the fridge for 20-30 minutes.
4. Break the bars into small squares. Shape the dough into little balls and press until they are flat. Add 1-2 pieces of chocolate and seal into the ball.
5. Arrange on the cookie sheet and bake for about 15 minutes. Remove and enjoy!

Chocolate Macaroon Cookies with Coconut

Servings: 20
Macros: 1 g Net Carbs | 2.2 g Prot. | 7 g Fat | 77 Cal.

Ingredients:

- Almond flour – 1 cup
- Coconut flour – 3 tbsp.
- Cocoa powder – .25 cup
- Baking powder – .5 tsp.
- Erythritol – .33 cup
- Shredded unsweetened coconut – .33 cup
- Salt – .25 tsp.
- Room temperature eggs – 2
- Coconut oil – .25 cup
- Vanilla extract – 1 tsp.

Preparation Method:

1. Line a baking tin with some aluminum foil.
2. Warm up the oven to reach 350°F.
3. Sift all of the dry fixings into a mixing container. Slowly add the wet components, mixing well.
4. Roll the dough into small balls and place on the prepared pan – several inches apart.
5. Bake for 15 to 20 minutes.
6. Sprinkle with the shredded coconut and enjoy.

Coconut Almond Cookies

Servings: 6
Macros: 2 g Net Carbs | 7 g Prot. | 25 g Fat | 271 Cal.

Ingredients:

- Almond flour – 1.25 cups
- Unsweetened shredded coconut – .5 cup
- Large eggs – 3
- Softened butter – 6 tbsp.
- Sugar substitute – .33 cup
- Almond extract – 1 tsp.
- Ground cinnamon – .25 tsp.
- Sea salt – .25 tsp.

Preparation Method:

1. Warm up the oven to reach 350°F.
2. Spritz a baking tin with some cooking oil spray.
3. Combine the sweetener of choice and softened butter.
4. One at a time, whisk and stir in the eggs until well incorporated.
5. Stir in the rest of the fixings – with the coconut added last.
6. Drop by the spoonful onto the prepared baking sheet. Bake for 12 to 15 minutes. Cool on a wire rack before storing.

Coconut No-Bake Cookies

Servings: 20
Macros: -0- g Net Carbs | 3 g Prot. | 10 g Fat | 99 Cal.

Ingredients:

- Melted coconut oil – 1 cup
- Monk fruit sweetened maple syrup or your favorite – .5 cup
- Shredded unsweetened coconut flakes – 3 cups

Preparation Method:

1. Cut out a sheet of parchment paper and place on a cookie tray.
2. Combine all of the fixings.
3. Run your hands through some water from the tap and shape the mixture into small balls. Arrange them on the pan around one to two inches apart.
4. Press them down to form a cookie and refrigerate until firm.
5. You can prepare these into individual bags if you're an on-the-go kind of person. It will stay fresh covered for up to 7 days (room temperature). Store in the fridge for up to a month or frozen up to two months.

Cream Cheese Cookies

Servings: 75 – 4 each
Macros: 2 g Net Carbs | 4 g Prot. | 19 g Fat | 204 Cal.

Ingredients:

- Surkin:1 or your favorite sugar substitute – .75 cup
- Softened cream cheese – 4 oz.
- Butter – 1 cup
- Egg – 1
- Coconut flour – .5 cup
- Almond flour – 2 cups

Preparation Method:

1. Warm up the oven to 350°F.
2. Cream the sweetener and butter until fluffy. Fold in the cream cheese and add the egg. Stir in both flours and mix in the vanilla.
3. Chill the prepared dough for a minimum of four hours.
4. Squeeze the dough into a cookie press. You can also roll it into a log and slice.
5. Bake 8-10 minutes – pressed cookies or 10-12 minutes – sliced.

Ginger Snap Cookies

Servings: 1
Macros: 2.2 g Net Carbs | 2.25 g Prot. | 6.7 g Fat | 74 Cal.

Ingredients:

- Ground cloves – .25 tsp.
- Nutmeg – .25 tsp.
- Salt – .25 tsp.
- Almond flour – 2 cups
- Ground cinnamon – .5 tsp.
- Unsalted butter – .25 cup
- Vanilla extract – 1 tsp.
- Large egg – 1

Preparation Method:

1. Warm up the oven temperature to 350°F.
2. Whisk the dry components in a mixing bowl. Blend in the rest of the ingredients into the dry mixture using a hand blender. The dough will be stiff.
3. Measure out the dough for each cookie and flatten with a fork or your fingers.
4. Bake for about 9-11 minutes or until browned.

Nut Butter Cookies

Servings: 10
Macros: 7 g Net Carbs | 5 g Prot. | 22 g Fat | 235 Cal.

Ingredients:

- Almond butter – 8.8 oz.
- Powdered Erythritol – .25 cup
- Egg – 1
- Salted butter – .25 tsp.
- Raw coconut butter – .25 cup

Preparation Method:

1. Warm up the oven to 320°F. Prepare a cookie sheet with a sheet of parchment paper.
2. Using a double boiler, melt the almond butter. Take it from the heat and stir in the Erythritol, salt, and egg. Fold until well mixed.
3. Break into 10 segments and roll into balls. Place on the prepared pan and flatten with a fork or your hand.
4. Bake for 12 minutes until browned to your liking.

Orange Walnut Cookies

Servings: 10
Macros: 4 g Net Carbs | 7 g Prot. | 17 g Fat | 137 Cal.

Ingredients:

- Walnut halves – 8 oz.
- Minced orange – zested – 3 tbsp.
- Eggs – 1
- Stevia drops – 20
- Cinnamon – garnish
- Shredded coconut – garnish

Preparation Method:

1. Set the oven temperature to about 320°F. Toast the walnuts for about 10 minutes until browned. Add them to a food processor. Toss in the rest of the fixings and continue blending until it's smooth.
2. Shape into ten balls and slightly flatten. Drizzle with some shredded coconut.
3. Bake for 40 minutes. Cool on the rack a few minutes and add to a platter to finish cooling. Store in an air-tight container and enjoy any time.

P B & J Cookies

Servings: 6
Macros: 5 g Net Carbs | 18 g Fat | 9 g Prot. | 209 Cal.

Ingredients:

- Egg – 1
- Sugar substitute – stevia – .5 cup
- Creamy Keto-friendly peanut butter – .66 cup
- Sugar-free strawberry preserves – .33 cup
- Almond flour – .33 cup
- Sea salt – .25 tsp.
- Baking powder – .25 tsp.
- Pure vanilla extract – .25 tsp.

Preparation Method:

1. Warm up the oven to 350°F. Spray a cookie sheet with a spritz of cooking oil or a layer of parchment paper.
2. Whisk the egg and combine with the stevia and peanut butter. When it's creamy, add the flour, salt, baking powder, and vanilla.
3. Mix well and shape into small balls. Make an indention in each one and add 1 teaspoon of preserves.
4. Bake until browned (10-12 min.). Cool on a wire rack and serve.

Peanut Butter Cookies

Servings: 6
Macros: 2 g Net Carbs | 7 g Prot. | 14 g Fat | 160 Cal.

Ingredients:

- Almond butter/Natural peanut butter/ your favorite – .5 cup
- Coconut flour – .5 cup
- Sugar substitute/Maple syrup – .25 cup
- Egg – 1
- Pure vanilla extract – .25 tsp.
- Sea salt – 1 pinch

Preparation Method:

1. Warm up the oven until it reaches 350°F. Cut out a sheet of parchment paper to fit a metal baking tray or spritz with a misting of cooking oil spray.
2. Combine all of the fixings. Prepare using an electric mixer until a dough is formed. Shape into little balls for the cookies. Arrange on the baking tin. Use a fork and make a crisscross pattern on each one.
3. Bake until golden or about 14—16 minutes.

Strawberry Thumbprints

Servings: 16
Macros: 1 g Net Carbs | 2g Prot. | 9 g Fat | 95 Cal.

Ingredients:

- Almond flour – 1 cup
- Baking powder – .5 tsp.
- Coconut flour – 2 tbsp.
- Salt – .5 tsp.
- Cinnamon – .5 tsp.
- Sugar-free strawberry jam – 2 tbsp.
- Shredded coconut – 1 tbsp.
- Erythritol – .5 cup
- Whisked eggs – 2
- Coconut oil – 4 tbsp.
- Almond extract – .5 tsp.
- Vanilla extract – .5 tsp.

Preparation Method:

1. Set the oven temperature to 350°F. Cover a cookie tin with a sheet of parchment paper.
2. Whisk the dry fixings and make a hole in the middle. Combine and fold in the wet fixings to form a dough. Break it into 16 segments and roll into balls.
3. Arrange each one on the prepared cookie sheet and bake 15 minutes.
4. When done; cool completely, and add a dab of jam to each one with a sprinkle of coconut.

Chapter 4: Bar Cookies

You will find a tasty batch in one of these cookie bars.

Almond Pumpkin Seed Bars

Servings: 8
Macros: 3.8 g Net Carbs | 4.7 g Prot. | 25 g Fat | 261.5 Cal.

Ingredients:

- Almond flour – 1 cup
- Melted butter – divided – .25 cup
- Erythritol – divided – .25 cup
- Salt – .5 tsp.
- Almond butter – .25 cup
- Heavy cream – .25 cup
- Cinnamon – .5 tsp.
- Maple extract – 1 tsp.
- Xanthan gum – .25 tsp.
- Toasted pumpkin seeds – .5 cup
- Also Needed: 8 x 8-inch baking pan

Preparation Method:

1. Warm up the oven until it reaches 400°F. Prepare a baking pan with a layer of parchment paper.
2. Combine 1/4 cup of the butter, salt, almond flour, and 1 tablespoon of the Erythritol. Mix well.
3. Press the crust (above) into the baking pan or dish. Bake for 12 to 15 minutes. Transfer to the countertop and let it cool.
4. Use a blender to combine the almond butter, rest of the melted butter, xanthan gum, maple extract,

cinnamon, and heavy cream. Blend until smooth and creamy. Scoop it into the prepared crust and top with the toasted pumpkin seeds.
5. Store in the fridge for a minimum of two hours—overnight is best.
6. Slice into 8 squares.

Cheesecake Mocha Bars

Servings: 16
Macros: 3.24 g Net Carbs | 6.1 g Prot. | 21.2 g Fat | 232 Cal.

Ingredients for the Brownie Layer:

- Vanilla extract – 2 tsp.
- Unsalted butter – 6 tbsp.
- Large eggs – 3
- Almond flour – 1.5 cups
- Hershey's Baking Cocoa or your favorite – .5 cup
- Erythritol – 1 cup
- Salt – .5 tsp.
- Instant coffee – .5 tbsp.
- Baking powder – 1 tsp.

Ingredients for the Cream Cheese Layer:

- Erythritol – .5 cup
- Large egg – 1
- Softened cream cheese – 1 lb.
- Vanilla extract – 1 tsp.
- Also Needed: 8x8-inch baking pan

Preparation Method:

1. Set the oven temperature to 350°F. Lightly grease or spray the pan.
2. Combine the wet fixings starting with the vanilla and butter. Next, mix in the eggs.
3. In another container, combine the dry ingredients and whisk with the wet fixings. Set aside 1/4 cup of the batter for later. Pour the mixture into the pan.

4. Mix the cream cheese (room temperature) with the rest of the ingredients for the second layer. Spread it on the sheet of brownies.
5. Use the reserved batter as the last layer (will be thin). Bake 30-35 minutes. When cooled, slice the cheesecake bars, and enjoy.

Chia Bars

Servings: 14
Macros: 1.5 g Net Carbs | 2.5 g Prot. | 11 g Fat | 121 Cal.

Ingredients:

- Toasted almonds – .5 cup
- Coconut oil – divided – 1 tbsp. (+) 1 tsp.
- Erythritol – 4 tbsp. – divided
- Butter – 2 tbsp.
- Heavy cream – .25 tsp.
- Liquid stevia – .25 tsp.
- Vanilla extract – 1.5 tsp.
- Unsweetened & shredded coconut flakes – .5 cup
- Chia seeds – .25 cup
- Coconut cream – .5 cup
- Coconut flour – 2 tbsp.
- Also Needed: Food Processor

Preparation Method:

1. Add the toasted almonds into the food processor and pulse until crumbly.
2. Toss in 1 tablespoon of the coconut oil and 2 tablespoons of the Erythritol. Continue processing until you have almond butter. (Now you have another new usable product.)
3. Warm up a pan and add the butter, heavy cream, Erythritol, stevia, and vanilla. Stir until they're bubbly and fold in the almond butter. Stir to blend.
4. In a blender, grind the chia seeds to make a powdery mix. In another pan, toast the coconut flakes and mix with the chia seeds. Melt the coconut cream in a separate skillet.

5. Now, combine all of the fixings and add the melted coconut cream, flour, and coconut oil. Store in the fridge for one hour.
6. When it's ready, slice into squares and store in the refrigerator.

Coconut Cashew Protein Bars – No-Bake

Servings: 12
Macros: 8.3 g Net Carbs | 11 g Prot. | 16 g Fat | 212 Cal.

Ingredients:

- Coconut butter – .5 cup
- Cashew butter – .25 cup
- Coconut oil – .25 cup
- Ground flaxseed – .66 cup
- Protein powder –your favorite – 1.33 cups
- Coconut or cashew milk – .25 cup
- Liquid stevia coconut drops – .5 tsp.
- Optional Topping: Unsweetened coconut flakes
- Also Needed: 8 x 8-inch baking dish

Preparation Method:

1. Soften the coconut butter, cashew butter, and coconut oil in the microwave or saucepan. Stir to incorporate and set aside to cool.
2. In another container, whisk the flaxseed and protein powder. Stir in the milk.
3. Taste test the cashew/coconut mixture for sweetness and adjust accordingly. Combine the rest of the fixings, mixing well.
4. Portion into 12 servings and enjoy.

Coconut Chia Bars

Servings: 6 bars
Macros: 3.5 g Net Carbs | 4 g Prot. | 14 g Fat | 164 Cal.

Ingredients

- Water – .5 cup
- Chia seeds – 4 tbsp.
- Coconut oil – 1 tbsp.
- Confectioners Swerve – 1 tbsp.
- Vanilla extract – .25 tsp.
- Shredded dried coconut meat – unsweetened – 1 cup
- Cashews – .5 cup
- Also Needed: 9 x 9 cookie sheet

Preparation Method:

1. Set the oven temperature to 350°F.
2. Soak the seeds 15 minutes until gel-like, and mix with the coconut, oil, swerve, and vanilla extract. Lastly, add the cashews.
3. Line the mixture, using parchment paper, onto the baking tin. Press until it is about a 3/4-inch thickness, and bake for 45 minutes.
4. Slice into six bars and enjoy!

Coconut Cream Brownies

Servings: 6
Macros: 2 g Net Carbs | 3 g Prot. | 17 g Fat | 175 Cal.

Ingredients:

- Raw unsweetened cocoa powder – .25 cup
- Coconut flour – .25 cup
- Sugar substitute – .5 cup
- Sea salt – 1 pinch
- Melted coconut butter – .75 cup
- Coconut cream – .33 cup
- Melted butter or coconut oil – 2 tbsp.
- Egg – 1
- Pure vanilla extract – 1 tsp.
- Baking soda – .25 tsp.
- Also Needed: 9 x 3-inch loaf pan

Preparation Method:

1. Lightly spritz the pan with cooking oil spray. Warm up the oven to 350°F.
2. Whisk the cocoa powder, coconut flour, sugar substitute, salt, and baking powder in a large mixing container.
3. Mix the coconut butter, butter, and coconut cream. Whisk in the vanilla and egg.
4. Fold in the dry components and mix well. Arrange in the loaf pan. Bake until a toothpick inserted in the center comes out clean or about 20 minutes.
5. Cool at room temperature. Slice into squares and enjoy.

Dark Chocolate Brownies

Servings: 16
Macros: 4 g Net Carbs | 8 g Fat | 3 g Prot. | 76 Cal.

Ingredients:

- Cream cheese – 6 tbsp.
- Eggs – 3
- Coconut oil – 3 tbsp.
- Cocoa powder – heaping 2 tbsp.
- Almond flour – .25 cup
- Coconut flour – .25 cup
- Baking soda – .25 tbsp.
- Truvia – 9 packets
- Almond milk – .5 cup
- Vanilla extract – 1 tsp.
- Salt – 1 pinch

Preparation Method:

1. Warm up the oven to 375°F.
2. Lightly spritz the baking tin with cooking oil spray.
3. Whisk the eggs, cream cheese, coconut oil, almond milk, and vanilla extract.
4. In a separate container mix the dry fixings (almond flour, cocoa powder, coconut flour, Truvia, baking soda, and a pinch of salt).
5. Combine everything and scoop into the cake pan. Bake for about half an hour and chill before serving.

Easy Brownie in a Mug

Servings: 1
Macros: 5 g Net Carbs | 35 g Prot. | 15 g Fat | 310 Cal.

Ingredients:

- Granulated sweetener – 1 tbsp.
- Eggs – 2
- Heavy cream – 1 tbsp.
- Protein powder – 1 scoop

Preparation Method:

- You will love this one. Just add the eggs, cream sweetener, and protein powder into the chosen mug. Mix well.
- Place the cup in the microwave for one minute. Remove with caution and enjoy.

Peanut Butter Protein Bars

Servings: 12 bars
Macros: 3 g Net Carbs | 7 g Prot. | 14 g Fat | 172 Cal.

Ingredients:

- Coconut or olive oil – for the pan
- Almond meal – 1.5 cups
- Chunky peanut butter – Keto-friendly – 1 cup
- Egg whites – 2
- Almonds – .5 cup
- Cashews – .5 cup
- Also Needed: Baking pan

Preparation Method:

1. Warm up the oven ahead of time until it reaches 350°F. Spritz a baking dish lightly with coconut or olive oil.
2. Combine all of the fixings and add to the prepared dish.
3. Bake 15 minutes and cut into 12 pieces once they're cooled.
4. Store in the fridge to keep them fresh.

Pumpkin Bars with Cream Cheese Frosting

Servings: 16
Macros: 2 g Net Carbs | 3 g Prot. | 13 g Fat | 139 Cal.

Ingredients:

- Large eggs – 2
- Coconut oil – .25 cup
- Pumpkin puree – 1 cup
- Cream cheese – 2 oz.
- Almond flour – 1 cup
- Vanilla extract – 1 tsp.
- Gluten-free baking powder – 2 tsp.
- Erythritol sweetener blend – .66 cups
- Pumpkin pie spice – 1 tsp.
- Sea salt – .5 tsp.

Ingredients for the Frosting:

- Powdered Erythritol – .5 cup
- Heavy cream – 1 tbsp. – optional
- Softened cream cheese – 6 oz.
- Vanilla extract – 1 tsp.
- Also Needed: 1 – 9 x 9 – baking pan

Preparation Method:

1. Warm up the oven until it reaches 350°F. Cover the baking pan with parchment paper.
2. In a double boiler or microwave, melt the coconut oil and cream cheese.
3. Combine the vanilla, eggs, cream cheese, and puree using a hand mixer until smooth (medium-speed).

4. Whisk the dry fixings (salt, pie spice, baking powder, sweetener, and flour).
5. Mix all the ingredients with the mixer until just combined and pour into the pan.
6. Bake for 20 to 30 minutes. Cool completely.
7. Prepare the frosting with each of the ingredients when the bars are cooled. If it's too thick, just add a little cream or milk.
8. Slice into 16 equal portions. Enjoy any time.

Tart Lemon-Lime Bars

Servings: 16
Macros: 2 g Net Carbs | 3.2 g Prot. | 19.2 g Fat | 192.3 Cal.

Ingredients:

- Almond flour – 1.5 cups
- Unsweetened shredded coconut for the crust – .5 cup
- Melted butter – divided – 1 cup
- Erythritol – .25 cup
- Freshly grated ginger – 1 tbsp.
- Lime – juice – .25 cup each
- Lime – zested – 1 tbsp.
- Lemon – juiced – .25 cup
- Egg yolks – 6
- Xanthan gum – .5 tsp.
- Plain gelatin – 2 tbsp.
- For the Garnish: Toasted shredded coconut – .25 cup
- Chopped fresh mint – 1 tbsp.

Preparation Method:

1. Cover an 8 x 8-inch pan with parchment paper. Warm up the oven to 350°F.
2. Mix the almond flour, ginger, Erythritol, 1/2 cup of the coconut, and 1/2 cup of melted butter. Press into the bottom of the baking dish. Bake until the crust is golden or for 10-12 minutes. Let it cool thoroughly.
3. Pour the rest of the butter into a pan using the low heat setting. Stir in the lime zest, lemon and lime juice.
4. Crack the eggs one by one. Separate and add the egg yolks. Continue to stir until thickened.
5. Transfer from the heat and add the gelatin and xanthan gum. Stir until it dissolves. Pour over the

cooked crust. Return the pan to the hot oven and bake for 15-18 minutes. The bars should be set in the center.

6. Cool the bars slightly before you garnish with some fresh mint and toasted coconut.
7. Slice into bars and store or serve.

Chapter 5: Cakes & Cheesecakes

Cakes

Berries & Cream Keto Cake with Brown Sugar Whipped Cream

Servings: 1
Macros: 8 g Net Carbs | 16 g Prot. | 65 g Fat | 671 Cal.

Ingredients for the Cake Batter:

- Large eggs – 2
- Torani or your favorite Sugar-free vanilla bean sweetener syrup – .25 cup
- Melted ghee – not hot – 2 tbsp.
- Room temperature organic cream cheese – 2 tbsp.
- Almond flour – .25 cup
- Mixed berries – raspberries/blueberries/strawberries/etc. – .25 cup

Ingredients for the Whipped Cream:

- Heavy whipping cream – .25 cup
- Sugar-free brown sugar syrup – ex. Torani/your preference – .5 tbsp.

Preparation Method:

1. Toss the eggs, cream cheese, ghee, and sweetener in a single-serving blender. Scrape into a regular-size mug. Stir in the flour and berries. Place in the microwave for four minutes.

2. Rinse out the single-serve blender and add the cream and brown sugar sweetener. Puree until it stiffens – it's whipped cream.
3. Once the cake has finished baking, just let it cool for a minute and add the cream.

Chocolate Lava Cake

Servings: 4
Macros: 3 g Net Carbs | 8 g Prot. | 17 g Fat | 189 Cal.

Ingredients:

- Unsweetened cocoa powder – .5 cup
- Melted butter – .25 cup
- Eggs – 4
- Sugar-free chocolate sauce – .25 cup
- Sea salt – .5 tsp.
- Ground cinnamon – .5 tsp
- Pure vanilla extract – 1 tsp.
- Stevia – .25 cup
- Also Needed: Ice cube tray & 4 ramekins

Preparation Method:

1. Pour one tablespoon of the chocolate sauce into four of the tray slots and freeze.
2. Warm up the oven to 350°F. Lightly grease the ramekins with butter or a spritz of oil.
3. Mix the salt, cinnamon, cocoa powder, and stevia until combined. Whisk in the eggs – one at a time. Stir in the melted vanilla extract and butter.
4. Fill each of the ramekins halfway and add one of the frozen chocolates. Cover the rest of the container with the cake batter.
5. Bake for 13-14 minutes. When they're set, place on a wire rack to cool for about five minutes. Remove and put on a serving dish.
6. Enjoy by slicing its molten center.

Chocolate Roll Cake

Servings: 12
Macros: 3 g Net Carbs | 5 g Prot. | 25 g Fat | 275 Cal.

Ingredients for the Mix:

- Almond flour – 1 cup
- Melted butter – 4 tbsp.
- Eggs – 3
- Psyllium husk powder – .25 cup
- Cocoa powder – .25 cup
- Coconut milk – .25 cup
- Sour cream – .25 cup
- Erythritol – .25 cup
- Vanilla – 1 tsp
- Baking powder – 1 tsp.

Ingredients for the Filling:

- Cream cheese – 8 oz. pkg.
- Butter – 8 tbsp.
- Sour cream – .25 cup
- Erythritol – .25 cup
- Stevia – .25 tsp.
- Vanilla – 1 tsp.

Preparation Method:

1. Warm up the oven to 350°F.
2. Combine each of the dry fixings and combine slowly with the wet components.
3. Mix well and spread the dough over a foil-covered baking tin. Bake for 12 to 15 minutes. Transfer to the counter to cool slightly to handle.

4. Prepare the filling. Spread the mixture over the dough and roll up your cake. Be sure to make it tight and enjoy.

Gingerbread – Slow Cooker

Servings: 10
Macros: 8.6 g Net Carbs | 9.1 g | Prot. | 24.8 g Fat | 223 Cal.

Ingredients:

- Almond/sunflower seed flour – 2.25 cups
- Coconut flour – 2 tbsp.
- Salt – .25 tsp.
- Ground cloves – .5 tsp.
- Swerve sweetener – .75 cup
- Ground ginger – 1.5 tbsp.
- Dark cocoa powder – 1 tbsp.
- Ground cinnamon – .5 tsp.
- Baking powder – 2 tsp.
- Large eggs – 4
- Melted butter – .5 cup
- Water or almond milk – .66 cup
- Freshly squeezed lemon juice – 1 tbsp.
- Vanilla extract – 1 tsp.
- Recommended Size: 6-quarts

Preparation Method:

1. Spritz the cooker with some cooking oil spray.
2. Whisk the all of the flour, salt, cloves, baking powder, cinnamon, ginger, sweetener, and cocoa powder in a large mixing container.
3. Blend in the eggs, melted butter, almond milk or water, vanilla extract, and lemon juice.
4. Empty the batter into the slow cooker and cook until set – approximately
2.5 to 3 hours.
5. Garnish as desired and enjoy, but count those carbs.

Lemon Cake

Servings: 8
Macros: 5.2 g Net Carbs | 7.6g Prot. | 32.6 g Fat | 350 Cal.

Ingredients:

- Coconut flour – .5 cup
- Baking powder – 2 tsp.
- Almond flour – 1.5 cups
- Swerve (or) *Pyure* All-purpose – 3 tbsp.
- Xanthan gum – .5 tsp. optional
- Whipping cream – .5 cup
- Melted butter – .5 cup
- Zest & juice – 2 lemons
- Eggs – 2

Ingredients for the Topping:

- *Pyure* all-purpose/Swerve – 3 tbsp.
- Lemon Juice – 2 tbsp.
- Boiling water – .5 cup
- Melted butter – 2 tbsp.
- Recommended: 2-4-quart slow cooker

Preparation Method:

1. For the Cake: Mix the dry ingredients in a container. Whisk the egg, lemon juice and zest, butter, and whipping cream. Combine all of the fixings and mix well. Scoop out the dough into the prepared slow cooker.
2. For the Topping: Mix all of the topping ingredients in a container, and empty over the batter in the cooker.
3. Place the lid on the cooker for two to three hours on the high setting.
4. Serve warm with some fresh fruit or whipped cream.

Mocha Pudding Cake – Slow Cooker

Servings: 6
Macros: 3.76 g Net Carbs | 9.29 g Prot. | 29.8 g Fat | 413.5 Cal.

Ingredients:

- Coconut oil spray or butter – for the cooker
- Finely chopped unsweetened chocolate – 2 oz.
- Butter – large chunks – .75 cup
- Heavy cream – .5 cup
- Vanilla extract – 1 tsp.
- Instant coffee crystals – 2 tbsp.
- Almond flour – 1.33 cup
- Unsweetened cocoa powder – 4 tbsp.
- Salt – .125 tsp.
- Large eggs – 5
- Stevia Erythritol granulated sweetener – .66 cup
- Low-carb whipped cream/ice cream – Optional
- Recommended: 4-6-quart slow cooker

Preparation Method:

1. Grease the cooker with butter/spray.
2. Using the medium heat setting on the stovetop, melt the unsweetened chocolate and butter in a small pan. Whisk occasionally. Take it off of the burner and cool.
3. Whisk the heavy cream, vanilla extract, and coffee crystals in a small container.
4. Mix together the almond flour, cocoa, and salt in another dish.
5. Whip the eggs using a mixer (high-speed). Slowly add the sweetener when thickened. Beat on the high setting about five minutes.
6. Slowly, on the low setting, use the mixer to combine

the unsweetened chocolate mixture and butter –
adding it to the cake mixture.
7. Fold in the flour, salt, and cocoa mixture. Blend
    (medium speed), and add the coffee, cream, and
    vanilla ingredients.
8. Add the batter to the prepared slow cooker, and place
    a paper towel over the slow cooker top to absorb the
    moisture.
9. Secure the top and cook on low for 2.5 to 3.5 hours (4-
    quart cooker) or for 2-3 hours (6-quart cooker).
10. Test for doneness in the center at 160°F. The center
    will be a soft soufflé consistency with an outer cake-
    like appearance.
11. Enjoy, but remember to count the extra carbs.

Pumpkin Blondies

Servings: 12
Macros: 1.5 g Net Carbs | 2 g Prot. | 11 g Fat | 110 Cal.

Ingredients:

- Coconut oil – for the pan
- Egg – 1 large
- Softened butter – .5 cup
- Pumpkin puree – .5 cup
- Erythritol – .5 cup
- Almond flour – .25 cup
- Coconut flour – 2 tbsp.
- Cinnamon – 1 tsp.
- Pumpkin pie spice – .125 tsp.
- Liquid stevia – 15 drops
- Maple extract – 1 tsp.
- Chopped pecans – 1 oz.

Preparation Method:

1. Heat up the oven temperature to 350°F. Grease a baking pan with a spritz of coconut oil.
2. Using an electric mixer to blend the egg, butter, puree, and Erythritol.
3. Combine each of the flours with the pie spice, stevia, cinnamon, and maple extract.
4. Blend it all together and add to the awaiting tin. Sprinkle the top with pecans. Bake 20-25 minutes until the edges are lightly browned.

Raspberry Coconut Cake – Slow Cooker

Servings: 10
Macros: 6.7 g Net Carbs | 10.4 g Prot. | 32 g Fat | 362 Cal.

Ingredients:

- Unsweetened shredded coconut – 1 cup
- Almond flour – 2 cups
- Swerve sweetener – .75- 1 cup
- Large eggs – 4
- Powdered egg whites – .25 cup
- Salt – .25 tsp
- Baking soda – 2 tsp.
- Melted coconut oil – .5 cup
- Raspberries – fresh or frozen – 1 cup
- Coconut extract – 1 tsp.
- Almond or coconut milk – .75 cup
- Sugar-free dark chocolate chips – .33 cup
- Coconut oil or favorite cooking spray

- Recommended: 6-quart size

Preparation Method:

1. Spritz the inside of the slow cooker with some cooking oil spray.
2. Whisk the flour, sweetener, coconut, salt, baking soda, and powdered egg whites in a large mixing container.
3. Add the coconut or almond milk, eggs, coconut extract, and melted coconut oil. Stir well and fold in the chips and berries.
4. Spread the prepared batter into the cooker and cook on the low setting for three hours. Turn the unit off and let it cool.
5. Top with whipped cream and enjoy!

Raspberry Cream Cheese Coffee Cake – Slow Cooker

Servings: 12
Macros: 3.9 g Net Carbs | 7.5 g Prot. | 19.2 g Fat | 239 Cal.

Ingredients:

- Swerve sweetener – .5 cup
- Almond flour – 1.25 cups
- Salt – .25 tsp.
- Vanilla protein powder – .25 cup
- Coconut flour – .25 cup
- Baking powder – 1.5 tsp
- Large eggs – 3
- Water – .66 cup
- Organic butter – melted – 6 tbsp.
- Vanilla extract – .5 tsp.

Ingredients for the Filling:

- Powdered swerve sweetener – .33 cup
- Organic cream cheese – 8 oz.
- Large egg – 1
- Fresh raspberries – 1.5 cups
- Organic whipping cream – 2 tbsp.
- Suggested Size of Cooker: 6-quart

Preparation Method

1. Grease the insert of the cooker thoroughly and prepare the batter.
2. Combine the dry fixings. Stir in the melted butter, eggs, and water.
3. Prepare the filling. Whip the sweetener and cream

cheese until smooth. Whisk the whipping cream, vanilla extract, and egg until well mixed.

4. Assemble the cake using 2/3 of the batter into the prepared cooker.
5. Smooth the batter and add the cream cheese mixture. Sprinkle with the berries. Use a spoon to 'dot' the top of the cake mixture.
6. Prepare for three to four hours on the low setting or until the edges are browned. The filling may still have a little jiggle if shaken.
7. Turn off the cooker and remove the insert.
8. Let it cool before serving. It is also tasty served chilled.

Spice Cakes

Servings: 12
Macros: 3 g Net Carbs | 6 g Prot. | 27 g Fat | 277 Cal.

Ingredients:

- Salted butter – .5 cup
- Erythritol – .75 cup
- Eggs – 4 – divided
- Vanilla extract – 1 tsp.
- Ground clove – .25 tsp.
- Allspice – .5 tsp.
- Nutmeg – .5 tsp.
- Almond flour – 2 cups
- Baking powder – 2 tsp.
- Cinnamon – .5 tsp.
- Ginger – .5 tsp.
- Water – 5 tbsp.
- Also Needed: Cupcake tray

Preparation Method:

1. Heat up the oven temperature to 350°F. Prepare the baking tray with liners (12).
2. Mix the butter and Erythritol with a hand mixer. Once it's smooth, combine with 2 eggs and the vanilla. Add the rest of the eggs and mix well.
3. Grind the clove to a fine powder and add with the rest of the spices. Whisk into the mixture. Stir in the baking powder and almond flour. Blend in the water. When the batter is smooth; add to the prepared tin.
4. Bake for 15 minutes. Enjoy any time.

Strawberry & Cream Cakes

Servings: 5
Macros: 3.7 g Net Carbs | 30 g Fat | 6 g Prot. | 275 Cal.

Ingredients:

- Eggs – 3
- Cream cheese – 3 oz./6 tbsp.
- Baking powder – .25 tsp.
- Vanilla extract – .5 tsp.
- Erythritol – 2 tbsp.

Ingredients for the Filling:

- Strawberries – 10
- Heavy cream – 1 cup

Preparation Method:

1. Cover a baking sheet with parchment paper.
2. Break the eggs and which just the egg *whites*. Whisk to form stiff peaks.
3. In another dish; combine the cream cheese, egg *yolks*, vanilla extract, baking powder, and Erythritol.
4. Slowly add the egg mixtures together. Shape into cake forms and place on the lined baking tin.
5. Whip the heavy cream until thickened.
6. Bake for 25-30 minutes. Let them cool and add the berries and cream.

Zucchini Bread

Servings: 12
Macros: 13.8 g Net Carbs | 15.7 g Fat | 5 g Prot. | 174 Cal.

Ingredients:

- Almond flour – 1 cup
- Cinnamon – 2 tsp.
- Coconut flour – .33 cup
- Baking powder – 1.5 tsp.
- Optional: xanthan gum – .5 tsp
- Salt – .5 tsp.
- Baking soda – .5 tsp.
- Softened coconut oil or butter – .33 cup
- Eggs – 3
- Vanilla – 2 tsp.
- Pyure all-purpose – .5 cup

- Shredded zucchini
- Chopped pecans or walnuts – .5 cup
- Also Needed: 4x8 silicone bread pan

Preparation Method:

1. Combine the coconut and almond flour, salt, baking soda, and powder, cinnamon, and xanthan gum. Set aside for now.
2. Mix the oil, eggs, vanilla, and sugar in another dish. Combine the fixings.
3. Blend in the nuts and shredded zucchini. Scoop the batter into the prepared bread pan.
4. Arrange the cooker on the top rack (or on crunched up aluminum foil balls). You want it at least 1/2-inch from the bottom of the slow cooker.
5. Put the top on the cooker and prepare for three hours using the high-temperature setting.
6. Cool, wrap in foil, and place in the fridge. It is best when refrigerated.

Cheesecakes

Banana Split Cheesecake – No-Bake

Servings: 20
Macros: 6.7 g Net Carbs | 4.1 g Prot. | 30 g Fat | 302 Cal.

Ingredients for the Crust:

- Cinnamon – 2 tsp.
- Almond flour – 3 cups
- Swerve – .33 cup
- Melted butter – 1 cup

Ingredients for the Filling:

- Swerve confectioner's sugar – 1 cup
- Melted butter – 1 cup
- Cream cheese – 16 oz.

Ingredients for the Topping:

- Chopped banana – 1
- Sliced strawberries – 2 pints
- Lemon juice – 1 tbsp.
- Heavy whipping cream – 2 cups
- Gelatin – 1.5 tsp.
- Vanilla extract – 1 tsp.
- Swerve – 3 tbsp.
- Nuts – optional
- Water – 3 tbsp.
- Chocolate sauce – optional
- Also Needed: 9 x 13-inch pan

Preparation Method:

1. Combine the crust fixings and press together in the pan.
2. Mix the sweetener, melted butter, and cream cheese until creamy. Spread on top of the crust.
3. Combine the banana and strawberries in a mixing dish along with the lemon juice. Make the next layer.
4. Prepare the Topping: Combine the whipping cream and gelatin in the water and beat well. Blend in the vanilla extract and sweetener. Whip until it is creamy to cover and make the next layer.
5. Top with the chocolate sauce and nuts if you like it that way.

Cheesecake Cupcakes

Servings: 12
Macros: 2.1 g Net Carbs | 4.9 g Prot. | 20 g Fat | 204 Cal.

Ingredients:

- Butter – .25 cup – melted
- Almond meal – .5 cup
- Eggs – 2
- Softened cream cheese – 16 oz. pkg.
- Stevia or your favorite sweetener – .75 cup
- Vanilla extract – 1 tsp.

Preparation Method:

1. Warm up the oven until it reaches 350°F. Prepare a muffin tin with 12 paper liners.
2. Combine the butter and almond meal. Spoon into the cups to make a flat crust.
3. Whisk the vanilla, sweetener of choice, eggs, and cream cheese with an electric mixer until creamy. Scoop it in on top of the crust. Bake for 15-17 minutes.
4. Once they're done the cooking cycle, just remove and cool at room temperature. Store overnight or at least 8 hours.
5. Enjoy anytime for a delicious treat.

Individual Strawberry Cheesecakes

Servings: 4
Macros: 9 g Net Carbs | 8 g Prot. | 47 g Fat | 489 Cal.

Ingredients for the Crust:

- Almond flour – .5 cup
- Melted butter/coconut oil – 3 tbsp.
- Sugar substitute – your preference – .25 cup or Maple syrup

Ingredients for the Filling:

- Sugar substitute – 3 tbsp. or use Grade B maple syrup
- Strawberries – 6
- Cream cheese – 8 oz.
- Sour cream – .33 cup
- Pure vanilla extract – .5 tsp.

Ingredients for the Garnish:

- Strawberries – 4
- Fresh mint leaves

Preparation Method:

1. Combine the crust fixings in a mixing bowl. Blend well and divide into four small ramekins. Gently press with your fingers.
2. Prepare the filling in a food processor. Pulse until creamy smooth.
3. Divide it over the crust of each one and chill for an hour or until it's set.
4. Garnish with another berry if desired and serve. (Add the carbs for any added garnishes)

Lemon Mousse Cheesecake

Servings: 1
Macros: 1.7 g Net Carbs | 3.7 g Prot. | 30 g Fat | 277 Cal.

Ingredients:

- Lemon juice – 2 lemons approx. – .25 cup
- Cream cheese – 8 oz.
- Salt – .125 tsp.
- Lemon liquid Stevia – 1 tsp. or to your liking
- Heavy cream – 1 cup

Preparation Method:

1. Use a mixer to blend the lemon juice and cream cheese until it's creamy smooth. Add the remainder of the ingredients and whip until blended.
2. Taste test. Add to a serving dish and sprinkle with some lemon zest.
3. Refrigerate until you are ready to enjoy.

New York Cheesecake Cupcakes

Servings: 12
Macros: 14.7 g Net Carbs | 6.5g Prot. | 26.7 g Fat | 273 Cal.

Ingredients:

- Melted butter – 5 tbsp.
- Almond meal – .66 cup
- Cream cheese – 16 oz.
- Sour cream – .5 cup
- Swerve or another favorite – .75 cup
- Water – 2 tbsp.
- Heavy whipping cream – .25 cup
- Eggs -3
- Almond flour – 2 tbsp.
- Vanilla extract – 1.5 tsp.

Preparation Method:

1. Heat up the oven to reach 350°F. Prepare a 12-count muffin pan with paper liners.
2. Combine the butter and almond meal and spoon into the liners to form the crust.
3. Stir the sweetener and cream cheese until creamy. Blend in with the water and whipping cream. One at a time, add the eggs, stirring with each one.
4. Next, fold in the flour, sour cream, and extract. Spoon into the liners.
5. Bake for 15-18 minutes. Don't over-cook. The middle will be set when it's done. Cool on the countertop until room temperature. Then, store in the fridge overnight or a minimum of 8 hours.

Plain Cheesecake – No Bake

Servings: 6
Macros: 5 g Net Carbs | 6.9 g Prot. | 25 g Fat | 247 Cal.

Ingredients for the Crust:

- Melted coconut oil – 2 tbsp.
- Almond flour – 2 tbsp.
- Swerve Confectioner's/equivalent – 2 tbsp.
- Crushed salted almonds – 2 tbsp.

Filling Ingredients:

- Swerve confectioner's/equivalent – .25 cup
- Gelatin – 1 tsp.
- Cream cheese – 16 oz. pkg.
- Unsweetened almond milk – .5 cup
- Vanilla extract – 1 tsp.

Preparation Method:

1. Prepare the crust by combining all of the fixings under the crust section. Place one heaping tablespoon into the bottom of dessert cups. Press the mixture down and set aside.
2. Prepare the filling. Mix the sweetener and gelatin. Pour in the milk and stir (5 min.). Whip the vanilla beans and cream cheese with a mixer on medium until creamy. Add the gelatin mixture slowly until well incorporated.
3. Pour the mixture over the crust of each cup. Chill for three hours, minimum.

Chapter 6: Delicious Scones – Pies & Tarts

Pies & Scones

Blueberry Cream Pie

Servings: 16
Macros: 3 g Net Carbs | 5.4 g Prot. | 30 g Fat | 305 Cal.

Ingredients:

- Unsweetened shredded coconut – 1 cup
- Unsalted sunflower seeds – 1 cup
- Salt – .25 tsp.
- Softened butter – .25 cup

Filling Ingredients:

- Fresh or frozen blueberries – 1 cup
- Gelatin – 2.5 tsp/1 envelope
- Lemon juice – 2 tbsp.
- Water – 2 tbsp.
- Swerve sweetener – .75 tsp.
- Softened cream cheese – 16 oz.
- Liquid stevia – .5 tsp.
- Heavy cream – divided – 2 cups

Topping Ingredients:

- Heavy cream – 1 cup
- Blueberry mixture – reserved from the filling – .25 cup

- Vanilla liquid stevia – .5 tsp.
- Also Needed: 8 x 8 baking dish

Preparation Method:

1. Add all of the crust fixings in a food processor and pulse until combined. Coat the baking dish with a little non-stick cooking spray or a spritz of oil. Add the crust.
2. Process the lemon juice and berries in the food processor until chopped.
3. Pour the water into a pan. Once it starts boiling, add the gelatin, stir, and set aside to cool.
4. In a stand mixer, add the cream cheese, 3/4 cup of the berries, lemon stevia, and swerve – mixing until smooth. Stir in 1 cup of the heavy cream and blend two to three minutes. Drizzle with the gelatin and mix. Pour into the crust.
5. Add the other cup of heavy cream along with the rest of the berries and blend on the high setting in the mixture to form the topping.
6. Decorate the pie with the filling and chill in the fridge for two or three hours (overnight is best).
7. When ready to eat, decorate with a few berries.

Blueberry Scones

Servings: 12
Macros: 4 g Net Carbs | 2 g Prot. | 8 g Fat | 133 Cal.

Ingredients:

- Baking powder – 2 tsp.
- Almond flour – 1.5 cups
- Stevia – .5 cup
- Vanilla – 2 tsp.
- Raspberries – .75 cup
- Eggs – 3

Preparation Method:

1. Warm up the oven to 375°F. Prepare a baking pan with a piece of parchment paper.

2. Whisk the baking powder, flour, stevia, and vanilla. Whisk the egg and add it to the mixture. Fold in the raspberries.
3. Add the batter to the prepared baking sheet and place in the oven.
4. Bake 15 minutes and remove the scones from the oven.
5. Cool slightly before serving.

Creamy Lime Pie

Servings: 8
Macros: 4.2 g Net Carbs | 7 g Prot. | 38.6 g Fat | 386 Cal.

Ingredients:

- Almond flour – 1.5 cups
- Erythritol – divided – .5 cup
- Salt – .5 tsp
- Melted butter – .25 cup
- Heavy cream – 1 cup
- Egg yolks – 4
- Freshly squeezed key lime juice – .33 cup
- Lime zest – 1 tbsp.
- Cubed cold butter – .25 cup
- Vanilla extract – 1 tsp.
- Xanthan gum – .25 tsp.
- Sour cream – 1 cup
- Cream cheese – .5 cup

Preparation Method:

1. Warm up the oven to 350°F. Melt the butter in a pan.
2. Mix the salt, half or 1/4 cup of the Erythritol, and the almond flour. Slowly add the butter. Blend and press into a pie platter.
3. Bake in the preheated oven for 15 minutes. Remove when it's lightly browned. Let it cool.
4. In another saucepan, combine the egg yolks, heavy cream, rest of the Erythritol, lime zest and juice. Simmer over medium heat for 7 to 10 minutes or until it starts to thicken.
5. Take the pan from the heat and add the xanthan gum, vanilla extract, cold butter, cream cheese, and sour cream. Whisk until smooth.

6. Scoop into the cooled pie shell. Cover and place in the fridge for four hours. For best results, leave it overnight.

Pumpkin Cheesecake Pie

Servings: 8
Macros: 6 g Net Carbs | 10 g Prot. | 44 g Fat | 460 Cal.

Ingredients:

- Almond flour – 1.75 cups
- Cinnamon – .5 tsp.
- Swerve – 3 tbsp.
- Melted butter – 1 stick

Ingredients for the Filling:

- Swerve – .66 cup
- Pumpkin puree – .66 cup
- Vanilla extract – .5 tsp.
- Cinnamon – .5 tsp.
- Allspice – .125 tsp.
- Nutmeg – .25 tsp.
- Large eggs – room temperature – 2
- Room-temperature – cream cheese – 16 oz.
- Also Needed: 9-inch pie plate

Preparation Method:

1. For the Crust: Combine the sweetener, cinnamon, and almond flour in the baking dish. Melt and stir in the butter. Press the fixings together.
2. For the Filling: Mix the sweetener, vanilla, and cream cheese with an electric mixer. When smooth blend in the eggs, pumpkin, nutmeg, cinnamon, and allspice.
3. Scrape the filling into the prepared crust. Bake 35-40 minutes.
4. Remove when the filling is firm. Set aside to cool down on a wire rack.
5. Chill overnight or at least a few hours before serving in equal portions.

Tarts

Cheesecake Tarts

Servings: 12
Macros: 2.8 g Net Carbs | 9 g Prot. | 16 g Fat | 175 Cal.

Ingredients for the Crust:

- Melted butter – 3 tbsp.
- Almond flour – .75 cup

Ingredients for the Filling:

- Room temperature cream cheese – 12 oz.
- Egg – 1
- Erythritol – .25 cup
- Fresh lemon juice – 1 tbsp.
- Vanilla extract – 1 tsp.

- Salt – .25 tsp.

Ingredients for the Toppings:

- Sugar-free strawberry jam – .25 cup
- Blueberries – .25 cup

Preparation Method:

1. Warm up the oven temperature to reach 350°F. Cover a cupcake tin with paper or silicone cupcake liners.
2. Melt the butter and mix with almond flour. Stir well until it becomes crumbly.
3. Press the crust mixture into each liner. Bake until they are golden brown (5 to 8 min.).
4. Prepare the filling. Combine the cream cheese with a hand mixer until softened. Whisk the egg and add to the mixture with 1/4 cup of Erythritol sweetener. Next, add 1 teaspoon of vanilla extract, 1 tablespoon of fresh lemon juice and 1/4 teaspoon of salt and mix one last time.
5. Scoop out the filling into the baked crusts and bake for about 20 minutes.
6. Let them cool on the counter for about ten minutes. Garnish each one with a tsp. of the jam. Add a portion of fresh fruit over that. Try three to four berries for each mini cake.

Dark Chocolate Tart

Servings: 4
Macros: 6 g Net Carbs | 13 g Prot. | 46 g Fat | 490 Cal.

Ingredients for the Crust:

- Coconut flour – 1 cup
- Flaxseed meal – .25 cup
- Sugar substitute – your preference – 3 tbsp. or to taste
- Butter – .5 cup
- Egg whites – 4

Ingredients for the Filling:

- Raw unsweetened cocoa powder – .5 cup
- Heavy cream – 1 cup
- Gelatin powder – 2.5 tsp.
- Sugar substitute – .25 cup or to taste
- Pure vanilla extract – 1 tsp.
- Sliced pistachios – .25 cup

Preparation Method:

1. Warm up the oven to 375°F. Prepare a pie pan or small tart pan with a spritz of cooking spray.
2. Combine the crust fixings in a food processor. Pulse until well mixed. Press into the prepared pan/pans. Bake for 15 minutes.
3. When it is ready, put the pan on a rack to cool.
4. Prepare the filling by combining all of the components except for the pistachios into a blender. Mix well until creamy smooth.
5. Add the mixture to the prepared crust/crusts. Cover the pie with a sheet of plastic wrap. Place it in the fridge for about 2 hours. It should be firm.

6. When ready to serve, just add the sliced pistachios and enjoy.

Lemon Custard Tarts

Servings: 2
Macros: 2 g Net Carbs | 17 g Prot. | 95 g Fat | 954 Cal.

Ingredients for the Crust:

- Unsalted melted butter – 3 tbsp.
- Almond meal – .75 cup
- Optional: Dried lavender flowers – .5 tsp.
- Sugar-free Vanilla bean sweetener syrup – ex. Torani – 1 tbsp.

Ingredients for the Filling:

- Freshly squeezed lemon juice – .5 cup
- Large egg yolks – 4
- Grated zest of lemon – 3
- Unsalted butter – melted – .5 cup.
- Sugar-free vanilla syrup- your brand preference – .25 – .5 cup
- Also Needed: 2 crème Brule dishes – 4.5-inch x 1.25 thick

Preparation Method:

1. Heat up the oven to 375°F. Lightly spritz the dishes with some ghee or butter.
2. Prepare the Crust: If you're using the flowers, grind them into a fine dust with a mortar and pestle. Combine with the 3 tablespoons of melted butter and almond flour. Press into the bottom of the two dishes.
3. Bake until the tops start browning (10 min.). Transfer to the counter to cool.

4. Make the Filling: Use a food processor or blender to mix the lemon juice, sweetener, egg yolks, lemon zest and rest of the butter. Scoop into a saucepan (med-low) and simmer about 15 minutes or until it's pudding-like.
5. When ready, pour the filling over the two crusts. Secure a layer of plastic wrap over each one and refrigerate overnight.

Mini Chocolate Avocado Tarts

Servings: 4
Macros: 5 g Net Carbs | 11 g Prot. | 33 g Fat | 367 Cal.

Ingredients:

- Almond flour – 2 tbsp.
- Stevia or your choice – 1 tbsp.
- Large egg white – 1
- Flax meal – .25 cup
- Natural peanut butter/almond butter – 4 tbsp.
- Butter/coconut oil – 2 tbsp.
- Also Needed: 4 small tart tins

Ingredients for the Top Layer:

- Medium avocado – 1
- Unsweetened cocoa powder – 4 tbsp.
- Stevia sugar substitute – .25 cup.
- Heavy cream – 2 tbsp.
- Pure vanilla extract – .5 tsp.

Preparation Method:

1. Heat up the oven to reach 350°F.
2. Combine 1 tablespoon of the stevia, flax meal, almond flour, and egg white.
3. Press the crust into the tins. Bake for until they're golden brown or about 8 minutes. Transfer to the countertop and cool.
4. Melt the butter and peanut butter in a small saucepan (med-low heat). Stir well and divide into each of the shells. Chill for 30 minutes.
5. Mix the cocoa powder, avocado, stevia, vanilla extract, and heavy cream in a food processor or blender.

6. Take the tarts out of the fridge and garnish with the blended avocado mixture. Place it back in the refrigerator for an hour for a minimum of one hour. Serve.

Pumpkin Pecan Tarts

Servings: 2
Macros: 9 g Net Carbs | 19 g Prot. | 45 g Fat | 530 Cal.

Ingredients for the Crust:

- Almond flour – .5 cup
- Butter – melted – 2 tbsp.
- Cinnamon – 1 tsp.
- Salt – 1 pinch

Ingredients for the Filling:

- Ricotta cheese – .5 cup
- Pumpkin puree – .5 cup
- Pumpkin pie spice – .25 tsp.
- Cinnamon – 1 tsp.
- Vanilla extract – .5 tsp.
- Salt – A pinch
- So Nourished Erythritol – 2 tbsp.

- Whole egg – 1 (+) Egg white – 1

Ingredients for the Topping:

- Pecans – 16
- Sugar-free maple syrup

Preparation Method:

1. Heat up the oven to 350°F.
2. Combine the crust fixings in a mixing container. Mix well and press into mini tartlet pans (4.5-inch pans). Bake for about 10 minutes and set aside to cool.
3. Prepare the Filling: Combine all of the fixings. Pour into the cooled shells. Bake for 20 minutes (on a baking tin).
4. Remove and add some pecans to the tops. Place them back in the oven for 10 more minutes. The tops may be a little jiggly – but set.
5. Let them cool slightly and drizzle with the syrup of choice and a portion of whipped cream.

Chapter 7: Frozen Desserts

Ice cream never tasted so good—and they're Ketogenic!

Blueberry No-Churn Ice Cream

Servings: 4
Macros: 3 g Net Carbs | 2 g Prot. | 15 g Fat | 153 Cal.

Ingredients:

- Heavy whipping cream – 1 cup
- Fresh blueberries – .25 cup
- Sour cream or Crème Fraiche – .25 cup
- Beaten egg yolk – 1
- Pure vanilla extract – 2 tsp.

Preparation Method:

1. Use a hand mixer to whip the Crème Fraiche.
2. In another bowl, whip the heavy cream to form stiff peaks.
3. Carefully, fold them together. Puree the berries in a blender or food processor until smooth and creamy.
4. Combine the egg, with the puree, and vanilla. Combine all of the fixings until just combined.
5. Add to a loaf pan and freeze for 2 hours. Stir about every 30 minutes.
6. Enjoy anytime!

Butter Pecan Ice Cream

Servings: 4
Macros: 1 g Net Carbs | 3 g Prot. | 24 g Fat | 230 Cal.

Ingredients:

- Chopped pecans – .5 cup
- Xanthan gum – .125 tsp.
- Egg yolks – 2
- Pure vanilla extract – 1 tsp.
- Sugar substitute – .25 cup
- Butter- 2 tbsp.
- Heavy cream – 1 cup

Preparation Method:

1. Use the medium heat setting to melt the butter in a saucepan. Whisk in the cream. Stir in the sugar substitute and xanthan gum. Whisk well until combined and pour into a metal container to cool.
2. Next, slowly add the eggs using a hand mixer. Fold in the pecans and vanilla.
3. Place the container in the freezer for at least four hours – stirring every hour or so.
4. Remove from the freezer and serve with a few chopped pecans for the topping.

Chocolate Ice Cream

Servings: 4
Macros: 4.75 g Net Carbs | 1.75 g Prot. | 22.5 g Fat | 231 Cal.

Ingredients:

- Heavy whipping cream – 1 cup
- Powdered swerve/Erythritol confectioners – .33 cup
- Unsweetened cocoa powder – 1.5 tbsp.
- Vanilla extract – .5 tsp.
- Large egg yolks – 2

Preparation Method:

1. Warm up a saucepan using the medium-high heat setting. Stir in the whipping cream and swerve. Once it starts to boil; lower the heat setting to simmer.
2. Stir in the cocoa powder and mix well. Remove most of the chunks.
3. In another container, whisk the egg yolks and vanilla. Set to the side.
4. Once the mixture (step 1) has thickened, remove it from the burner to cool for about five minutes. Slowly combine the cream mixture to the yolks. Whisk with a hand mixer or a fork until it forms a frothy top.
5. Place in the freezer for 4-6 hours. Check several times. If it freezes overnight, you may want to let it sit out for a few minutes to be easier to scoop out of the container.

Chocolate Shakes

Servings: 2
Macros: 7 g Net Carbs | 4 g Prot. | 47 g Fat | 210 Cal.

Ingredients:

- Coconut milk – 4 oz.
- Heavy whipping cream – .75 cup
- Natural sweetener – swerve – 1 tbsp.
- Vanilla extract – .25 tsp.
- Unsweetened cocoa powder – 2 tbsp.

Preparation Method:

1. Empty the cream into a cold metal bowl. Use your hand mixer and cold beaters to form peaks.
2. Slowly add the milk into the cream. Add the rest of the fixings.
3. Stir well and portion into two glasses. Chill in the freezer one hour before serving. Tip: Stir a couple of times if possible.

Mint Chocolate Chip Shake

Servings: 2
Macros: 11 g Net Carbs | 4 g Prot. | 21 g Fat | 274 Cal.

Ingredients:

- Full-fat coconut milk – 1 cup
- Unsweetened dark chocolate – diced – 2 tbsp.
- Mint leaves – .5 cup
- Pitted avocado – .5 of 1
- Pure vanilla extract – 1 tsp.
- Sugar substitute or maple syrup – 1 tbsp.
- Ice – .5 cup

Preparation Method:

1. Combine each of the fixings in a high-speed blender (such as a NutriBullet). Pulse until smooth.
2. Serve immediately.

3. Tip: Add more ice if you like a thicker shake.

Peanut Butter Caramel Milkshake

Servings: 1
Macros: 5 g Net Carbs | 8 g Prot. | 35 g Fat | 365 Cal.

Ingredients:

- Coconut milk – 1 cup
- Ice cubes – 7
- Sugar-free salted caramel syrup – 2 tbsp.
- Natural peanut butter – 2 tbsp.
- MCT Oil – 1 tbsp.
- Xanthan gum – .25 tsp.

Preparation Method:

1. Combine each of the ingredients in a blender.
2. Mix well and serve in a chilled glass.

Pudding Pops

Servings: 1
Macros: 1.2 g Net Carbs | 2.8 g Prot. | 10.3 g Fat | 122 Cal.

Ingredients:

- Gelatin – 1 tsp.
- Vanilla extract – 1 tsp.
- Coconut/almond milk – from a carton – 1 cup
- Cocoa powder – 2 tbsp.
- Cream cheese – 6 oz.
- Liquid stevia – 20 drops
- Erythritol – powder – 1 tbsp.

Preparation Method:

1. Prepare a saucepan over low heat and add the milk. Mix in the gelatin slowly to dissolve. Remove from the burner when it starts steaming. Pour into a spouted container such as a measuring cup.
2. Combine the remainder of the fixings and use a blender to mix well.
3. Pour into a popsicle mold. Freeze for two hours – minimum.
4. Enjoy whenever that sweet urge strikes.

Pumpkin Ice Cream

Servings: 2
Macros: 3 g Net Carbs | 8 g Prot. | 20 g Fat | 250 Cal.

Ingredients:

- Butter – 1 tbsp.
- Chopped pecans – .25 cup
- Stevia – 1 tbsp.
- Cottage cheese – .25 cup
- Pumpkin puree – .25 cup
- Erythritol – .25 cup
- Egg yolks – 2
- Coconut or almond milk – 1 cup
- Pumpkin spice – 1 tsp.
- Xanthan gum – .25 tsp.

Preparation Method:

1. Warm a saucepan and add the butter and pecans. Cook for 8 to 10 minutes.
2. Blend the rest of the fixings in a blender
3. Add the mixture to an ice cream machine. Garnish with the pecans and serve.

Smoothie in a Bowl

Servings: 1
Macros: 4 g Net Carbs | 35 g Prot. | 35 g Fat | 570 Cal.

Ingredients:

- Almond milk – .5 cup
- Spinach – 1 cup
- Heavy cream – 2 tbsp.
- Low-carb protein powder – 1 scoop
- Coconut oil – 1 tbsp.
- Ice – 2 cubes

Ingredients for the Toppings:

- Walnuts – 4
- Raspberries – 4
- Chia seeds – 1 tsp.
- Shredded coconut – 1 tbsp.

Preparation Method:

1. Add a cup of spinach to your high-speed blender. Pour in the cream, almond milk, ice, and coconut oil.
2. Blend for a few seconds until it has an even consistency, and all ingredients are well combined. Empty the goodies into a serving dish.
3. Arrange your toppings or give them a toss and mix them together. Of course, make it pretty and alternate the strips of toppings.

Chapter 8: Delicious Smoothies

Smoothies are delicious for breakfast too!

Almond Lover Smoothie

Servings: 1 – 16 oz.
Macros: -0- g Net Carbs | 12 g Prot. | 23 g Fat | 511 Cal.

Ingredients:

- Medium banana – 1
- Almond milk – 8 oz. – 1 cup
- Plain non-fat Greek yogurt – .33 cup
- Cooked oats – .33 cup
- Almond butter – 2 tbsp.
- Almonds – 5

Preparation Method:

1. Measure all of the fixings into the cup of your NutriBullet or favorite high-speed machine.
2. Pour the milk up to the max-fill line. Blend until it is smooth and creamy.

Blackberry Cheesecake Smoothie

Servings: 1
Macros: 6.7 g Net Carbs | 6.4 g Prot. | 53 g Fat | 515 Cal.

Ingredients:

- Extra-virgin coconut oil – 1 tbsp.
- Fresh/frozen blackberries – .5 cup
- Water – .5 cup
- Coconut milk/heavy whipping cream – .25 cup
- Full-fat cream cheese or creamed coconut milk – .25 cup
- Sugar-free vanilla extract – .5 tsp.
- Liquid stevia – if desired – 3-5 drops

Preparation Method:

1. Toss all of the fixings into your blender.
2. Next, pulse until the mixture until it is smooth and frothy.
3. Add a few ice cubes and enjoy it in a chilled glass.

Blueberry – Banana Bread Smoothie

Servings: 2
Macros: 4.7 g Net Carbs | 3.1 g Prot. | 23.3 g Fat | 270 Cal.

Ingredients:

- Chia seeds – 1 tbsp.
- Golden flaxseed meal – 3 tbsp.
- Vanilla unsweetened coconut milk – 2cups
- Blueberries – .25 cup
- Liquid stevia – 10 drops
- MCT oil – 2 tbsp.
- Xanthan gum – .25 tsp.
- Banana extract – 1.5 tsp.
- Ice cubes – 2-3

Preparation Method:

1. Combine all of the ingredients into a blender.
2. Wait a few minutes for the seeds and flax to absorb some of the liquid.
3. Pulse for 1-2 minutes until well combined, and the texture you choose. Lastly, add the ice to your preference.

Blueberry – Coconut Chia Smoothie

Servings: 3
Macros: 11.3 g Net Carbs | 6.2 g Prot. | 21.1 g Fat | 249 Cal.

Ingredients:

- Coconut – .5 cup
- Unsweetened cashew or almond milk – 1 cup
- Frozen blueberries – 1 cup
- Ground chia seed – 2 tbsp.
- Full-fat Greek yogurt or almond milk – 1 cup
- Sweetener (equal to 2 tbsp. sugar) your choice
- Coconut oil – 2 tbsp.
- Optional: Cubes of ice -2-3

Preparation Method:

1. Carefully measure the ingredients and put them into your blender.
2. Mix until creamy smooth. Serve in three chilled glasses.

Blueberry & Kefir Smoothie

Servings: 2
Macros: 6.6 g Net Carbs | 3.9 g Prot. | 50 g Fat | 476 Cal.

Ingredients:

- Coconut milk kefir – 1.5 cups
- Fresh or frozen blueberries – .5 cup
- MCT oil – 2 tbsp.
- Water (+) ice cubes – .5 cup
- Sugar-free vanilla extract 1-2 tsp. or pure vanilla powder – .5 tsp.

Optional Ingredients:

- Collagen powder – 2 tbsp.
- Liquid stevia/your choice – 3-5 drops

Preparation Method:

1. Toss all of the ingredients into your blender
2. Pulse until the fixings are all mixed.
3. Serve in chilled glasses and enjoy your healthy choice!

Chocolate & Mint Smoothie

Servings: 1
Macros: 6.5 g Net Carbs | 5 g Prot. | 40 g Fat | 401 Cal.

Preparation Method:

Ingredients:

- Medium avocado – .5 of 1
- Coconut milk – .25 cup
- Unsweetened cashew/almond milk – 1 cup
- Swerve/Erythritol – 2 tbsp.
- Cocoa powder – 1 tbsp.
- Fresh mint leaves – 3-4
- MCT oil – 1 tbsp.
- Ice cubes – 2-3
- Optional: Coconut milk or whipped cream

Preparation Method:

1. Mix all of the ingredients in your blender.
2. Add ice cubes, as many as you like. Add the topping if preferred.
3. Serve and enjoy!

Chocolate Smoothie

Servings: 1 large
Macros: 4.4 g Net Carbs | 34.5 g Prot. | 46 g Fat | 570 Cal.

Ingredients:

- Large eggs – 2
- Almond or coconut butter – 1-2 tbsp.
- Extra-virgin coconut oil – 1 tbsp.
- Coconut milk or heavy whipping cream – .25 cup
- Chia seeds – 1-2 tbsp.
- Cinnamon – .5 tsp.
- Plain or chocolate whey protein – .25 cup
- Stevia extract – 3-5 drops
- Unsweetened cacao powder – 1 tbsp.
- Water – .25 cup
- Ice – .5 cup
- Vanilla extract – .5 tsp.

Preparation Method:

1. Add the eggs along with the rest of fixings into the blender.
2. Pulse until frothy. Add to a chilled glass and enjoy.

Cinnamon Roll Smoothie

Servings: 1
Macros: 0.6 g Net Carbs | 26.5 g Prot. | 3.25 g Fat | 145 Cal.

Ingredients:

- Almond milk – 1 cup
- Vanilla protein powder – 2 tbsp.
- Vanilla extract – .25 tsp.
- Cinnamon – .5 tsp.
- Sweetener – 4 tsp.
- Flax meal – 1 tsp.

- Ice – 1 cup

Preparation Method:

1. Combine all of the fixings in a blender. Add the ice last.
2. Blend on the high setting for 30 seconds until thickened.

5-Minute Mocha Smoothie

Servings: 3
Macros: 4 g Net Carbs | 3 g Prot. | 16 g Fat | 176 Cal.

Ingredients:

- Unsweetened almond milk – 1.5 cups
- Coconut milk – from the can – .5 cup
- Vanilla extract – 1 tsp.
- Instant coffee crystals – regular or decaffeinated – 1 tsp.
- Erythritol blend/granulated stevia- 3 tbsp.
- Unsweetened cocoa powder – 3 tbsp.
- Avocado – 1

Preparation Method:

1. Use a sharp knife to slice the avocado in half. Scoop the center out and discard the pit. Dice the avocado and add it along with the rest of the ingredients into the blender.
2. Mix well until smooth and serve.

Raspberry Avocado Smoothie

Servings: 2
Macros: 4 g Net Carbs | 2.5 g Prot. | 20 g Fat | 227 Cal.

Ingredients:

- Ripe avocado – 1
- Lemon juice – 3 tbsp.
- Water – 1.33 cups
- Frozen unsweetened raspberries/or choice of berries – .5 cup
- Your preference sugar equivalent – 1 tbsp. (+) 1 t.

Preparation Method:

1. Blend all of the components in a blender until creamy smooth.
2. Empty the smoothie into two chilled glasses and enjoy!

Raspberry Chocolate Cheesecake Smoothie

Servings: 1
Macros: 7 g Net Carbs | 6.9 g Prot. | 54 g Fat | 512 Cal.

Ingredients:

- Frozen or fresh raspberries – .33 cup
- Coconut milk/heavy whipping cream – .25 cup
- Full-fat cream cheese/creamed coconut milk – .25 cup
- Unsweetened cacao powder – 1 tbsp.
- Extra-virgin coconut oil – 1 tbsp.
- Water – .5 cup
- Liquid stevia extract – 3-5 drops – optional

Preparation Method:

1. Place all of the goodies for your smoothie in a blender.
2. Blend until frothy and smooth. Pour into a chilled glass and relax.

Strawberry Almond Smoothies

Servings: 2
Macros: 7 g Net Carbs | 15 g Prot. | 25 g Fat | 304 Cal.

Ingredients:

- Heavy cream – .5 cup
- Unsweetened almond milk – 16 oz.
- Stevia to taste
- Frozen unsweetened strawberries – .25 cup
- Whey vanilla isolate powder – 2 tbsp.

Preparation Method:

1. Combine each of the fixings into a blender.
2. Puree until smooth. Add a small amount of water to thin the smoothie.

Vanilla Smoothie

Servings: 1
Macros: 4 g Net Carbs | 12 g Prot. | 64 g Fat | 651 Cal.

Ingredients:

- Mascarpone full-fat cheese – .5 cup
- Large egg yolks – 2
- Water – .25 cup
- Coconut oil – 1 tbsp.
- Ice cubes – 4
- Liquid stevia 3 drops
- Pure vanilla extract – .5 tsp.
- Optional Topping: Whipped cream

Preparation Method:

1. Combine each of the ingredients in a blender until smooth.
2. Add the whipped cream for a special treat but add the carbs if any.

Conclusion

Thank you for choosing the Keto Desserts Cookbook. I hope you have enjoyed each and every recipe! The next step is to decide which tempting treat you should choose first. Just sit down and make a shopping list of all of the items you want to prepare.

Stay determined—and stand by your goals during your transition to Ketosis. Follow the instructions and recipe methods. Before long, you will be able to quickly scan other recipes and know before you finish reading how healthy they are for you and your family. Consider a few of the benefits you can achieve by following the Keto techniques:

- You will experience improved thinking skills.
- You can lower your blood pressure.
- Diabetes and prediabetes are improved using the program

The most significant benefit, though, is: *you are not hungry*.

Finally, if you found this book useful in any way, a review on Amazon is always appreciated!

Index for the Recipes

Chapter 2: Puddings & Scrumptious Candy

Puddings

Candy Treats

Delicious Fat Bombs

Allspice Almond Fat Bombs
Almond Butter Fat Bombs
Almond – Choco Fat Bombs
Blackberry Coconut Fat Bombs
Blueberry Cream Cheese Fat Bombs
Bulletproof Fat Bombs
Cacao Coconut Fat Bombs
Chocolate Fat Bombs
Chocolate Peanut Butter Fat Bombs
Chocolate Peppermint Fat Bombs
Coconut Macaroons Fat Bombs
Coffee Fat Bombs
Craving Buster Fat Bombs
Dark Chocolate Fat Bombs
Dark Chocolate Raspberry Fat Bombs
Lemonade Fat Bombs
Maple Almond Fudge Fat Bombs
Pistachio & Almond Fat Bombs
Raspberry Coconut Bark Fat Bombs
Stuffed Pecan Fat Bomb

Chapter 3: Cookies Galore

Amaretti Cookies
Chocolate Cookies
Chocolate Chip Cookies
Chocolate Coconut Cookies
Chocolate-Filled Peanut Butter Cookies
Chocolate Macaroon Cookies with Coconut
Coconut Almond Cookies
Coconut – No-Bake Cookies
Cream Cheese Cookies
Ginger Snap Cookies
Nut Butter Cookies
Orange Walnut Cookies
P B & J Cookies

Peanut Butter Cookies
Strawberry Thumbprints

Chapter 4: Bar Cookies

Almond Pumpkin Seed Bars
Cheesecake Mocha Bars
Chia Bars
Coconut Cashew Protein Bars – No-Bake
Coconut Chia Bars
Coconut Cream Brownies
Dark Chocolate Brownies
Easy Brownie in a Mug
Peanut Butter Protein Bars
Pumpkin Bars with Cream Cheese Frosting
Tart Lemon-Lime Bars

Chapter 5: Cakes & Cheesecakes

Cakes

Berries & Cream Keto Cake with Brown Sugar Whipped Cream
Chocolate Lava Cake
Chocolate Roll Cake
Gingerbread – Slow Cooker
Lemon Cake
Mocha Pudding Cake – Slow Cooker
Pumpkin Blondies
Raspberry Coconut Cake – Slow Cooker
Raspberry Cream Cheese Coffee Cake – Slow Cooker
Spice Cakes
Strawberry & Cream Cakes

Zucchini Bread

Cheesecakes

Banana Split Cheesecake – No-Bake
Cheesecake Cupcakes
Individual Strawberry Cheesecakes
Lemon Mousse Cheesecake
New York Cheesecake Cupcakes
Plain Cheesecake – No-Bake
Raspberry Cheesecake

Chapter 6: Delicious Scones – Pies & Tarts

Pies & Scones

Blueberry Cream Pie
Blueberry Scones
Creamy Lime Pie
Pumpkin Cheesecake Pie

Tarts

Cheesecake Tarts
Dark Chocolate Tart
Lemon Custard Tarts
Mini Chocolate Avocado Tarts
Pumpkin Pecan Tarts

Chapter 7: Frozen Desserts

Blueberry No-Churn Ice cream
Butter Pecan Ice Cream
Chocolate Ice Cream
Chocolate Shakes
Mint Chocolate Chip Shake
Peanut Butter Caramel Milkshake
Pudding Pops

Pumpkin Ice Cream
Smoothie in a Bowl

Chapter 8: Delicious Smoothies

Almond Lover Smoothie
Blackberry Cheesecake Smoothie
Blueberry Banana Smoothie
Blueberry Coconut Chia Smoothie
Blueberry & Kefir Smoothie
Chocolate Mint Smoothie
Chocolate Smoothie
Cinnamon Roll Smoothie
5-Minute Smoothie
Raspberry & Avocado Smoothie
Raspberry Chocolate Cheesecake Smoothie
Strawberry Almond Smoothies
Vanilla Smoothie

31904516R10111

Made in the USA
Middletown, DE
03 January 2019